Also by Richard Ben Cramer

What It Takes
Joe DiMaggio: The Hero's Life
What Do You Think of Ted Williams Now?
Ted Williams: The Seasons of the Kid
How Israel Lost

BEING POPPY

A PORTRAIT OF
George Herbert Walker Bush

RICHARD BEN CRAMER

SIMON & SCHUSTER
New York   London   Toronto   Sydney   New Delhi

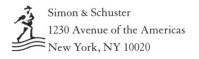 Simon & Schuster
1230 Avenue of the Americas
New York, NY 10020

First Simon & Schuster hardcover edition May 2013

SIMON & SCHUSTER and colophon are registered trademarks of Simon & Schuster, Inc.

For information about special discounts for bulk purchases, please contact Simon & Schuster Special Sales at 1–866–506–1949 or business@simonandschuster.com.

The Simon & Schuster Speakers Bureau can bring authors to your live event. For more information or to book an event contact the Simon & Schuster Speakers Bureau at 1–866–248–3049 or visit our website at www.simonspeakers.com.

Designed by Joy O'Meara

Manufactured in the United States of America

10   9   8   7   6   5   4   3   2   1

Library of Congress Cataloging-in-Publication Data is available.

ISBN: 978-1-4767-4541-1
ISBN: 978-1-4767-4559-6(ebook)

For John Ryan

A LETTER FROM THE PUBLISHER

RICHARD BEN CRAMER WAS working on this project when he died, suddenly and unexpectedly, in January 2013, at the age of sixty-two. He and his wife, Joan, were adapting this portrait of President George Herbert Walker Bush from Cramer's 1992 masterpiece, *What It Takes*, his 1,047-page account of the 1988 presidential campaign. The profile of Bob Dole in *What It Takes* is so well-crafted that it has been published separately as a short book. Now, with the publication of *Being Poppy*, President Bush, a modest and heroic man with a genius for friendship, receives his due.

Cramer spent six years writing *What It Takes*. From 1986 to 1992, he interviewed more than a thousand people, at campaign stops and in the hometowns of the candidates. He went to extremes to gain access to the candidates, gathering a detailed understanding of each character. "I know their dogs and their dead dogs," he said. "I know their families like a next-door neighbor would know them. As a consequence, when I was passed to the candidate, it was usually from his mother or his aunt or his wife's parents. It's a whole different way of coming onto their screens."

Cramer knew Joe Biden would never miss his son's football game, so he was sure to be at the school Saturday morning when the team was playing.

Walt Riker, press secretary to Bob Dole, realized he was dealing with someone unusual when Cramer started commenting on how good the cookies tasted back in the homes of Dole's Kansas relatives. "No one has ever researched the Senator to the extent that Cramer did," Riker said.

To penetrate Bush World, Cramer prevailed upon campaign director Lee Atwater to introduce him to George W. Bush, who eventually trusted Cramer enough to arrange some interviews with Poppy. (Atwater's final words to Cramer were "Now, don't fuck me.") In an interview with C-SPAN, Cramer said, "The real turning point with Bush came when George W. Bush, George Junior, brought me over to the residence for a backyard barbecue and horseshoes with the veep. Once the veep had drubbed me solidly in horseshoes, then I was on the map."

Cramer practiced a form of method journalism. He wouldn't write about a subject until he felt he could talk like him, empathize with him, share his outlook. He even tried to walk like his subjects. He *lived* with these people. He told me, "You love them. You hate them. They infuriate you. They delight you. You're worried about them. You're intensely connected to them." He named his cats Poppy and Bobster, after Bush and Dole.

By the time Cramer was done writing, the manuscript

weighed fifteen pounds. He called it "the refrigerator." He filled an entire guest bathroom in his Maryland home with discarded drafts and ultimately cut 75,000 words—a book in itself—with the help of his wife at the time, Carolyn White.

At Random House, Cramer's editor, David Rosenthal, presciently introduced the book to the sales force as an instant classic. Although the book did not have strong immediate sales, it attracted a cult following and ultimately influenced a generation of political journalists. Fifteen years after its publication, *New York Times Magazine* writer Matt Bai devoted a column to *What It Takes*, calling it "the most ambitious and riveting in a line of great campaign books." *Washington Post* writer Chris Cillizza and three reverent journalistic colleagues made a pilgrimage to Cramer's Maryland farmhouse to hear the now-legendary author's account of how he wrote his epic.

I was an associate editor at Random House at the time *What It Takes* was published and volunteered to write an article about the book for a magazine Random House circulated to bookstores. Richard was candid about the toll the endeavor had taken on his health. He was immobilized during the California primary, incapable of getting out of bed. In 1990, half of his face froze. His doctors said it was Bell's palsy. A year later, he weathered a case of pleurisy. "Writing is a deadly business," Cramer said wryly at the time. "It makes the stomach roil."

Cramer never intended to write a lot of books. He wanted to make each one count. From 1992 to 2000, he worked on *Joe DiMaggio: The Hero's Life*. With the help of his longtime literary agent, Philippa Brophy, he followed his editor, David Rosenthal, to Simon & Schuster, which published the book to wide acclaim and bestsellerdom. In 2004, Simon & Schuster published a short book on the Middle East, *How Israel Lost: The Four Questions*, a subject Cramer had first covered in the late 1970s as a Pulitzer Prize–winning foreign correspondent for *The Philadelphia Inquirer.*

Cramer had been a reporter since adolescence, growing up in Rochester, New York, where he was coeditor of his high school newspaper. His father, Robert "Brud" Cramer, described him as "single-minded" in his pursuit of a journalistic life, with the possible exception of wanting to play for the New York Yankees. At Johns Hopkins University, Cramer spent most of his time on the college newspaper, rising to the top position, followed by Columbia Journalism School and a stint at *The Baltimore Sun*, where he covered Maryland politics. In 1976, he was hired by *The Philadelphia Inquirer.* A year later, on a day's notice, he flew to Egypt to cover the Sadat/Begin peace talks. He was twenty-seven years old. "It was never the official version of geopolitical events," said John Carroll, who was then the *Inquirer's* metro editor. "He could spend days talking with Egyptian peasants and capture the problems of the Middle East through their eyes." Stuart Seidel, a college friend, remembers visiting Cramer in 1978 and walking the streets of Cairo with him. At one point, Cramer took Seidel's arm and urged him to stop, to take in the sounds and the aroma of spices from the open markets.

"What he did was tell stories," said his wife, Joan, who first met Cramer when she was a book review editor for *The San Francisco Examiner.* "He wasn't reductive about anything or anybody, and I think the stories to him conveyed a complexity that was more true than making a mere observation."

After publishing *How Israel Lost*, Cramer decided to write a book about New York Yankees slugger Alex Rodriguez. Richard became fascinated by Rodriguez in 2006, in the midst of what Cramer referred to as A-Rod's "season of woe." His ambition was to write an account of a baseball superstar's highs and lows through A-Rod's eyes, just as he had described the toll of a presidential campaign through the eyes of the 1988 candidates. ("What it takes," Cramer would tell people, "is your life.")

He was still working on the A-Rod project six years later. "Every day, he would get up and try to forward the project, whether that meant making phone calls or traveling," Joan said. "You spend every day trying to get closer to the subject and get people to trust you, and it just takes a lot of time."

Richard once shared a six-page introduction with me, about four years into the project. I sincerely told Richard they were the best six pages ever written about A-Rod. I didn't ask Richard many questions about his process, in part because I was in awe of his talent but also because I knew he was only going to turn in the manuscript when he was sure he had the story.

In a moment of frustration with his subject, he had told me that the conventional wisdom on baseball players and politicians is wrong. People think baseball players are heroes and that politicians are awful, he said, noting that he'd found the opposite to be true.

Perhaps that feeling brought the author back to George Herbert Walker Bush, one of the politicians he most admired. With

Joan's help, he spent many weeks cutting and pasting his favorite Bush passages from *What It Takes* into this edition. According to Joan, he was "all fired up about it, reading Bartlett and Steele's new book about the American oligarchy and thinking about how Bush was the last good Republican, how he raised taxes because it was good for the country even though it was political suicide."

Richard Ben Cramer died before he could write the introduction to this book, but Joan found this note from him, which he intended to be part of his opening:

George H. W. Bush had a firm idea about holding public office. He tried to do what was right. By the time he held any jobs where the decisions were his, this was an odd and outmoded idea.

—JONATHAN KARP

BEING POPPY

I

THEY WERE ALL KIDS aboard the *San Jacinto*. Just past his twentieth birthday, Lieutenant George Bush looked so young he didn't seem ready to operate a car, much less the biggest bomber aircraft in the Pacific fleet. He was only a year past winning his wings as the youngest flier in the Navy. He was tall and skinny, with a high forehead and wide-set eyes that looked out at the world with a precocious gravity from under soft and delicately curved brows. The rest of his face—the narrow cheeks and the line of his long, slender jaw—was hairless and smooth, saved from prettiness only by a generous, slightly cleft chin and the quick, lopsided, aw-heck grin that dismissed his own good looks and made him, so readily, one of the guys. Still, as he sat up from a slouch in his steel chair in the ready room, and peered at the coordinates on the board, then bent to his own course calculations, he had the same buckle-down, teen-in-a-hurry look his Andover masters saw two years before, when Captain Poppy had to hustle through a history quiz, to get out to practice for the Exeter game.

But today it was a job: one more crack at Chichi Jima. They'd gone at it yesterday but couldn't wipe out the target: a radio tower and four outbuildings. They ran into a hail of flak and lost a plane. Today was their last shot: the task force would be steaming south, right after the raid, out of the sector altogether, to link up with Admiral Halsey for the landings on the Palau Islands. The radio tower on Chichi was the Japanese link to the Palaus.

Bush grabbed his gear and started for the deck. He liked to get up there early to check over his plane . . . but Ted White stopped him on his way out: he'd been after Bush for weeks to take him along on a mission. Ted was a ship's gunnery officer, not a flier. Leo Nadeau was Bush's turret gunner. It was always Bush and Nadeau, and the radio man, Jack Delaney. They'd been a crew since they were stateside. But Ted was older than Bush, a family friend, a buddy of Poppy's Walker uncles, a Yale man like them, a good, quiet fellow. Bush would be glad to take him up . . . but why'd he have to pick today? Ted had to know, it was gonna be rough. . . . Still, Bush didn't like to say no to a friend. He told White to check it out with Skipper Melvin. But he'd better step on it!

That was one more mark of the mission's import: Don Melvin would fly lead today. Melvin was the squadron skipper, the man who taught them to do things with their bulky TBM Avengers that they never learned in flight school. The guys used to say they ought to win the Bent Nail—instead of the Iron Cross—for serving in his squadron, VT-51. D. J. Melvin liked catapult takeoffs and tight formations: he liked his pilots cool, clear-eyed, more levelheaded and determined than kids should have to be.

On deck now, Leo Nadeau got the word to stand down. An officer was going up in his place, "to check out the turrets." Leo knew that was bullshit. You check that stuff on deck. But he was just an enlisted man, so he stood down, as Ted White strapped into the turret on top, behind Bush, and Delaney climbed into his regular spot in the belly of the TBM.

Anyway, there wasn't time to argue: Bush had the plane in the catapult and they were off, pressed back against their seats by the rush, as the TBM climbed into formation—tight formation, the way Melvin liked it. They had an hour's run to the island and a linkup with planes from other ships. The sky was clear, hazy blue, just a few broken clouds—too few: there'd be no cover over Chichi.

They came in at fourteen thousand, then pushed over in a shallow dive to pick up speed before they got to attack altitude, eight thousand feet. They pushed into bombing dives, an angle of thirty-five degrees. They were falling against their shoulder belts. Leo Nadeau used to say the Avenger could fall faster than it could fly. The ground was rushing toward Bush, but the flak . . . black bursts of smoke all over the sky . . . the worst flak he'd ever seen. He was third man in. He aimed his plane's nose on the tail of the man ahead—Doug West—and pushed over. There was the tower, and Melvin's plane dropping straight for it, West and Bush after him. The buildings around the tower, communication buildings, had to be hit, if the skipper got the tower. . . . Bush was hung against his harness, his plane gaining speed as it fell, a ton of bombs racked below, his eyes locked on the gathering ground, eight thousand, seven, six . . . flak on all sides and above . . . he could see the walls of the buildings . . . just a minute now, and . . .

3

HE FELT A JARRING lurch, a crunch, and his plane leapt forward, like a giant had struck it from below with a fist. Smoke started to fill the cockpit. He saw a tongue of flame streaming down the right wing toward the crease. Christ! The fuel tanks!

He called to Delaney and White—*We been hit!* He was diving. Melvin hit the tower dead on—four five-hundred-pounders. West was on the same beam. Bush could have pulled out. *Have to get rid of these bombs. Keep the dive . . . a few seconds . . .*

He dropped on the target and let 'em fly. The bombs spun down, the plane shrugged with release, and Bush banked away hard to the east. No way he'd get to the rendezvous point with Melvin. The smoke was so bad he couldn't see his gauges. Was he climbing? *Have to get to the water.* They were dead if they bailed out over land. The Japs killed pilots. *Gonna have to get out*, Bush radioed the skipper, called to his crew. No answer. *Does White know how to get to his chute?* Bush looked back for an instant. *God, was White hit?* He was yelling the order to bail out, turning right rudder to take the slipstream off their hatch . . . had to get himself out. He leveled off over water, only a few miles from the island . . . *more, ought to get out farther . . . that's it, got to be now. . . .* He flicked the red toggle switch on the dash—the IFF, Identification Friend or Foe—supposed to alert any U.S. ship, send a special frequency back to his own carrier . . . no other way to communicate, had to get out *now*, had to be . . . *NOW.*

Wind of a hundred twenty miles an hour tore away his canopy, tore at him like the claws of a beast, ripped him back at the tail of his plane, which he HIT . . . and then it was quiet. . . . *Hope to God Sayer packed the damn chute right.*

By rote, he found the ripcord, and the chute opened, but it was torn. He was falling fast. He'd hit his head and chute on the tail stabilizer. He was bleeding. He had to get out of the chute . . . if he got tangled up in the water, he'd drown before he could get to his raft. *Where's the raft? Where's Delaney? And White? God, was White hit?* There were no chutes on the water in front, but he couldn't yank around to see the other side. His head hurt like hell. His hands scrabbled at the chute release, a question mark of steel he had to open. Where were Delaney and White? The water rushed up to grab him.

The water, green water, was over his head. He was out of the chute and it drifted away as he kicked up for air, air—green water—air. It was all he could see, no raft, just water and sky. . . . *Have to swim, swim where?* He was gulping water, coughing and gulping. He heard noise over him, a plane, an Avenger, *Melvin! Skipper!* He was diving for Bush. No, not for Bush . . . over there, diving and climbing and diving again to the same spot. The raft. *The raft!* Bush kicked and scrambled through the water. There it was. *Oh, God, let it inflate.* . . . He draped his arms on the side of the raft and hauled himself out of the green. Now there were other planes overhead, another Avenger, and fighters, Hellcats. The Avenger was diving—Doug West. He'd seen the blood on Bush's face, dropped a medical kit. Bush hand-paddled for it.

There was no paddle. There was no fresh water: the container on the raft had broken in the fall. Bush was paddling with both hands, puking from fear and sea water, bleeding from the head. He got the med-kit, and with a shaky left hand, swabbed at himself with iodine. He got out his .38 revolver and checked it. Fat lot of good it would do him. The wind was blowing him back to the beach. He had to keep splashing, beating the sea with his hands. If the Japanese got him, they'd kill him, for sure.

He scanned the rolling green horizon on all sides, the boundary of his fearful new world. No yellow rafts. Just air, green water. The planes were gone. They had to get back to the squadron, the carrier, the task force. They'd radio back his position. Probably had the news on the bridge already, and at his CIC, Combat Information Center. Someone would come back. There were three men out here somewhere. If he could just hold on, keep beating the water, stay away from the island, find White and Delaney, they'd have to come back. Then he remembered— the briefing: *this was the last chance . . . the task force was turning south this morning, down to the Palaus, out of the sector. . . .* They were not coming back. They knew he was down. But they were not coming back!

On the deck of the *San Jacinto*, word spread that someone was down. News leaked from the bridge, like it always did, but they never really knew until the planes came back. And here they were, circling into a string for the landing: the fighters looked all right, but only three Avengers . . . and they landed, one after the other: Skipper . . . West . . . Moore. Then they knew. And the pilots on deck took this news like they always did. What was there to say? Someone muttered: "Jesus . . . George Herbert Walker Bush."

THAT WAS HIS NICKNAME aboard the *San Jacinto*: George Herbert Walker Bush.

Everybody had a nickname. Stan Butchart was, naturally, Butch; Milt Moore, their first replacement pilot, was renamed Gracie, after the famous comedienne of the day; the hairless wardroom officer, D. E. Garrett, was called Skin; even the revered Skipper Melvin got a handle, in consequence of his bad overbite: behind his back he was Mortimer. That was the way it had to be on a ship like that: the *San Jacinto* was tiny for a carrier, just a flattop on a light cruiser hull, only thirty-three planes aboard. With just thirteen bomber pilots in the squadron, with so many hours together on missions and patrol, with their shared loss when one of their guys didn't come back, with so much endless waiting together, so many games of acey-deucy, volleyball in the hangar wells, sunning on the forecastle, movies on the hangar deck, so many mornings in the ready room, three meals a day in the wardroom, together, for week, after week, after week, every bit of that narrow life layered with familiarity, an accretion of common memory and private slang. So flying as fourth man in formation, directly below and behind the lead plane, was called "flying snifter," a term Bush invented. So the spot where they sunned, behind windbreaks on the forecastle, became the "front porch." And a certain kind of ice-cream sundae, available below-decks, became a "gee-dunk." (No one could remember why.)

It wasn't a bad way to spend a war. No officer on the *San Jacinto* ever handled a shovel, spent a night in a foxhole, or had to be deloused. There was a daily ship's paper with wire reports on the news of the world, and a phonograph in the wardroom with Glenn Miller records. Coffee and toast, with real butter, or peanut butter, was available in the wardroom twenty-four hours a day. Officers ate three meals on white tablecloths, served by stewards in white coats, who'd offer each dish on silver trays, from which the gentlemen could take what they wanted. They had foods unavailable at home: roast beef and steak for supper, bacon and eggs in the morning, fruit juice, cream for their coffee. The ship made its own ice cream. The ship's baker made bread daily. They had a pastry chef from the Hilton in New York, for pies, cakes, sweet rolls, crullers.

Withal, there was a brilliant clarity to the life, a sense of purpose and progress that was the greatest comfort to twenty-year-olds: they were out to beat the Japs; the Japs were evil, killers, yellow lesser-lives who started it all with a sneak attack. Hadn't the boys sailed into Pearl? They'd seen the evidence themselves! There were no shades of gray in the picture. They were a team, with a mission. They had a job, beyond survival. That was the only thing that made sense when a plane didn't come back . . . one of their thirteen, just gone. . . . What was there to say? The guy was gone. There was his chair. They didn't replace him right away. The chair would be there, empty, for weeks. Meanwhile, there was still the war. There was always, thank God, a job to do. Once, coming back from a mission over Guam, the bombers circled and settled on the deck, one after the other, all accounted for. But as Bush watched the fighters land, one of the pilots missed the trip wire. His plane spun over the slick steel, into a gun turret manned by four seamen. The gun crew was wiped out in a fiery instant, and there, just a few yards from Bush on deck, was the severed leg of a sailor. . . . George Bush, nineteen years old, just stared at the thing. . . . *The shoe is still on it.* . . . Then, the chief petty officer bellowed: "Awright, you bastards. We still got planes up there, and they can't land in this goddam mess." There was still, there was always, a job.

Problem was, on the bombing runs, they were never on their own, or even in the lead. They were such a small air group, they were always the tagalongs, joining a larger force from other ships. There were four carriers in their group and four groups in the task force. That meant hundreds of planes, and missions divvied up among the ships, according to a plan that no one seemed to know—no one on their ship, anyway. It was sobering: how huge was the war, and how small were they, their ship, their squadron, their own plane. Sometimes, it was hard to feel that what you did—you, your own mother's son—meant a good god-damn in the whole million-mauling maw of the war.

But not for Bush. Hell, he didn't have any doubts, you could see that. He said it, too: he liked being part of a team. Liked the *cahm-rah-deree* of his three-man plane. On shipboard, he seemed to know more of the enlisted men than other pilots did. The Navy tried to discourage that: too much fraternization could lead to a breakdown of discipline . . . chain of command, see. In the air, that pilot was the captain of his vessel: the Navy wanted a minimum of chat, and instant obedience from the crew. But Bush would chat about anything—airplanes, baseball, the food back home . . . his girlfriend back home. . . . Despite regulations, her name was painted on the side of the plane—*Barbara*.

It wasn't that he bucked the rules; he always accommodated

the rules. But his captaincy sat easy on him, and he didn't mind having fun. Sometimes, coming back from patrol, when the plane to relieve him was already in the air, Bush would get on the intercom and tell Delaney to drop a flare. So Delaney would cram a smoke flare down the tube, and when it hit the water, Bush would wheel the TBM around and throw it into a dive for the water, so his men could have a good time with their guns. In the ready room, after general quarters, if he wasn't on the first mission and running to his plane, he'd stand up from his seat in the second row and turn, always with a grin and a wave, and wander back to the enlisted men, with a "Hey, Tony . . . Jake . . ."

That was the thing they all saw about Bush: he was a good Joe, no stickler for rank. He was *not like that*. That was the point about the nickname: it was like calling a bald guy Curly . . . His four names, his boys' school slang, his Big-Family-Back-East roots . . . he was trying so hard to be *not that way*. He was so eager to be a *friend to all* . . . that they just had to stick him with it: George Herbert Walker Bush. . . .

WHAT THEY NEVER KNEW, what they couldn't have known, was how thoroughly Bush was trained to be Not Like That. It was the central tenet of Poppy's world in Greenwich, Connecticut. The Bushes were always Not That Way.

You see, they so easily could have been. After all, Grandfather Walker moved the family from St. Louis to play with the

Harrimans and Vanderbilts and Astors. Pops Walker had gone off to school at Stonyhurst, in England, with his valet (rhymed with "mallet"), and ever after had a taste for the life of the polo-and-ponies crowd. By the time Poppy came along, Gampy Walker not only had the Point, up in Maine, he also had the big shooting place, an old plantation in South Carolina, where the family used to gather for Christmas, and that palace out on Long Island, with the marble floors, the swimming pool, two butlers . . . you didn't often see two butlers, even in the thirties. Or, for that matter, two Rolls-Royces: Pops had one, and one for Grandmother. Ganny Walker never drove in her life. Not that she was happy about it. Her chauffeur, John, was the kind who was always talking. "Y'know, I don't think I'd like bein' President," John was saying one day in the Rolls. "I don't think I'd take th' job if they gave itta me, I wouldn't. . . ." Ganny Walker just cranked up the glass that walled off the driver's seat. "As if he ever could think," she said.

Still, there was a hint of Midwest breeze that lingered in the family air, in the vigor of their play, in their open, hard-knuckled talk about business. That was the difference between the Walkers and New York's forever-monied, the ownership class of America: Astor, Rockefeller, Ogden Phipps. (Ganny used to say, a bit breathlessly: "They own the very sidewalks that we walk on!") The Walkers were only a few years removed from operation of the biggest dry-goods business west of the Mississippi. It was only in the span of G. H. Walker's career that the family made the move from St. Louis, from the class of "good families" in the heartland who owned factories or stores, who actually made or sold merchandise, to the class of pure owners, who invested in such business. So the Walkers still had links with the few families in each town—Pittsburgh, Cleveland, Akron, Detroit—who somehow knew one another, from business or from school (back East), or from some cotillion long ago. . . . And so it was, when Pops Walker's children grew up, they married children from the good Midwest: Herbie Walker married Mary Carter, of St. Louis; Johnny married Louise Mead, Dayton; Jimmy wed Sarah Mitchell, Detroit; Lou married Grace White, from St. Louis; and, of course, Dottie married Prescott Bush, the son of an officer in the Buckeye Steel Castings Co., of Columbus, O.

In Pres she found the apotheosis of midwestern virtue. Prescott Bush spent the bulk of his adult life in the monied sanctum of the Harrimans themselves: he was a managing partner of Brown Brothers Harriman, private bankers to the owning class. He belonged to the clubs of New York's forever-monied. He lived among them in Greenwich (his daily commuting pal was a Rockefeller). But Pres was forever Not Like That. Couldn't care less for anything ritzy. One time he got roped into a cruise with Averell Harriman and Pops Walker on their new boat, *The Pawnee*, a hundred-fifty-foot miracle of shining brass and mahogany, fireplace in the salon, crew of a score or so . . . the best of everything afloat. Pres was bored to death, couldn't wait to get off. He never could stand a lot of fussy feeding and primping. What was the fun in that?

Of course, once Pres brought Dottie back from the Midwest, where he started his career, and took up his post in New York with the Harrimans and his father-in-law, there was help in the Bush house, too: a woman who cooked, and her husband, who drove the kids to Greenwich Country Day School, and then, too, an Irish maid. But the Bushes didn't talk about their "chauffeur," their "housekeeper." It was Alex and Antonina, or, to strangers, "lovely people . . . the couple who live with us . . ." The point was, it was Not Like That. They were . . . like family! Lizzie Larkin, the maid, just adored Pres, jumped up aflutter in the mornings, delighted to help him on with his coat. Late afternoons, just before train time, she'd burst into the library, to plump up the pillows and make right for Mr. Bush, shooing the kids away in her brogue: "Y' chidren slouchin' around here, and yer fath'r workin' all day hard. Ah! None of you'll be the gentleman yer fath'r is. Now, get out, and let me tidy here! He'll be home in a minute now!" The message was constant, day by day: their father was a man of important work. Someday, perhaps, they'd earn their own crowns. Meanwhile, the Bush house held no princes of the realm.

Sure enough, when Alex brought Mr. Bush home from the station, Pres would go straight to the library, where he'd listen to the radio news, and then to his favorite bandleader, Fred Waring. Then, it was supper, and off to another important meeting, number three-hundred-something for the year. Or back to the telephone closet for important calls: father was not to be disturbed. Seldom would Dottie and Pres spend two nights in a row out at dinners. Though their friends, the Harrimans, the Lovetts, Ellery James, invited them always, they eschewed the constant round of parties, the evening-dress-Park-Avenue scene.

Occasionally, Pres and Dottie hosted a dinner of their own, and the children were sent to the upper floor, while the flowers were arranged and the drinks table set up. But the family recalled these as stiff affairs. The real parties were Sunday afternoons, when Pres's pals from the Midwest would show: Neil Mallon from Cleveland, the Hurds from Chicago, Henry Isham from Chicago . . . or sometimes, the Howard brothers, Yale men, who could play four hands on one piano, and after spaghetti, there'd be singing on the porch. Pres loved to sing.

Practice with his quartet, or with the choir—now there was an evening of fun! He brought to the practice of singing the same talent and serious craft he required of himself on a golf course: he was not in it just to hack around. He'd sit on the morning train to New York, singing to himself, then writing down the notes, scoring a new harmony for his quartet to try later that week. When he and Dottie got their house in Florida, on the private Jupiter Island preserve, Pres abandoned the island's proper Episcopal church, and sang with the Presbyterian choir in Hobe Sound, on the mainland, with the tradesmen and their wives, who really loved to sing. But it wasn't just the singing: there was a statement in it, too. To be a Bush was to be unimpressed by money and its splendors; it was to be *not* a Mellon, or a Reed, and certainly not their acolyte; it was to be, pointedly, Not Like That.

The Ping-Pong table in the front hall in Greenwich was more than a statement about games: it was an explicit rejection of the lives ("Do lower your voice, dear. The servants will hear!") around them. Pres used to joke about the "economic royalists," and at the table, the children would hear his arch report to Dottie:

"The So-and-So's have a terrible problem. They've lost their *caretaker* in Bar Harbor! What's *worse* is the caretaker on Long Island won't go *up* to Bar Harbor! . . . What *ever* are they to do?"

Even the economic royalists at Walker's Point got to Pres, with their exclusive Sunday lobster suppers, and the pews at St. Ann's Church, up front, on the right, where no one but Walkers would presume to sit. For a few years, he summered instead at Fishers Island, in Long Island Sound, where things were Not That Way.

When Pres spoke well of a man, his admiration likely had to do with service rendered to society or its institutions. He didn't have much good to say about those for whom money was the goal. Of course, one wanted to have enough, as did he, to provide for the family. But after that, what was the point? His own father was a man of important service: founder of the Community Chest in Columbus, O. To be a Bush was to be of benefit: that was the legacy.

Pres came of age with the notion that he might become a lawyer, and somehow go into politics. But the Great War intervened, and when he came back from his captaincy in France (which was "quite exciting and, of course, a wonderful experience"), he hadn't time or temperament for three more years of law school. Anyway, he was to be a family man, so he started his career in business. But even as he worked his way to partner in the banking firm run by his father-in-law and Averell Harriman, he had the idea that service was the measure of a man. Even in the worst of the stock market slump, after all, when business was toughest, and the Harriman interests were being merged with the older firm of Brown Brothers & Co., Averell Harriman lent most of his time and talent to Franklin Roosevelt in the White House, and to the New Deal's boards and commissions. Pres was not yet asked to serve at that Harrimanesque altitude. But as soon as Brown Brothers Harriman & Co. dug out from the crash (and the partners got their accounts out of the red), Pres got elected to the Greenwich Town Meeting, where he served as Moderator for most of the next two decades.

He cut a fine figure there, too. He knew enough of Robert's Rules to keep order, but he wasn't a stickler for parliamentary niceties. He was never afraid to take the meeting in hand and guide it simply by his own sense of where it ought to go. "A good, firm show" was what he liked to run, and after all, who'd brook him? He was six-foot-four, with a full head of hair, deep-set blue-gray eyes, a man of great stature and athletic grace, with his beautiful Whiffenpoof bass voice, and a Cesar Romero thousand-candlepower smile that was devastating to women. He was imposing enough to keep the meeting on track without ever raising his voice; he never cut anyone short, always took a lively interest and large view of the town's affairs. The great thing about Mr. Bush, other members of the meeting used to say, was that *a man like that* would listen to everybody's point of view. Most of the town services he could well afford to do without. But that wasn't the point: he was giving something back, serving, as a man ought. So night after night, he was there at the meetings; Pres knew as much as anyone about the sewers and the sidewalks, and the public schools that his children would never attend.

WHERE WERE WHITE AND Delaney? Did they bail out over the island? Why didn't they wait? Did they think he wasn't gonna make the water? Delaney had to know. They *did* a water landing, *did it before.* . . . The TBM was spewing oil when they took off. Bush set it down on the water, gentle as a mother's kiss. They paddled away, all three in a raft, paddling for their lives as the plane went down and the bombs went off under the sea, and they all three—twenty years old and alive, Dear God, Alive!— whaled away at the water while they started to sing, Nadeau started to sing . . . *Sailing, sailing, over the bounding main* . . . till a destroyer fished them out, singing, alive. . . . Hah! . . . Nadeau'll remember. Nadeau'll tell them, Bush was good.

What did it matter? They weren't coming back. They had orders, heading south. They were leaving, they were gone. Half the pilots in the squadron were gone—forever. Now he knew what happened to them. They were good, too. But it *didn't matter.* It wasn't about *him.* That was the point . . . what was the point now? What did it matter?

There was his service. He was good. No water. So he died. *Dear God* . . .

PRES BUSH CHOSE ANDOVER for Pressie and George because he thought it the most democratic school. Pres himself had put in a few years at a public school in Columbus, with German children, Italians, Irish, Negroes. He always thought that a benefit, especially in politics. But his boys had known only the privileged preserve of Greenwich Country Day, so Pres chose a school that would be "broadening." In those days, Andover made a nice point of taking some scholarship boys who were "different." Andover styled itself not a standard boys prep, in the Eton-English mold, like Groton, or St. Paul's, safe green islands for the forever-rich to come of age in proper company and style. It was not like Choate, where they took you in for your name, and thereafter, by whatever means, helped you get through. No, on its own terms, Phillips Academy, Andover, Mass., old P.A., proudly, was Not That Way.

P.A. declared that its business was making the leaders of tomorrow. The place reeked of promise: great doings to come. The motto of the academy was *Finis origine pendet*, The End Depends upon the Beginning. Even thirteen-year-olds like Poppy Bush were encouraged to keep their sights on that end, that life of virtue and purpose.

The striving wasn't about scholarship: most of the study was rote. (In fact, classes were called "recitations.") And although the tweedy, absentminded headmaster, Dr. Claude M. Feuss, urged them over and over to read, to ponder "the great books, the deeper classics," the fact was, with sports and clubs, meals, chapel, recitations . . . there just wasn't time. Andover men (they were always *men*) were joiners, doers, men of action. Philosophic or political talk was all very well for "dicking" (bull sessions) at night in some fellow's room. But all the best fellows were "sound" in their beliefs—in other words, they thought pretty much what everybody ought to.

In fact, their politics weren't much different from those of their fathers in their mansions and boardrooms. The student newspaper, the *Phillipian*, hammered at Roosevelt's New Deal as "anti-democratic centralized government . . . anti-business . . . fuzzy headed theoretical nonsense." The problem with the New Dealers, of course, was they just weren't *sound*. As the paper opined, endorsing Landon over Roosevelt, the year before Poppy arrived, Roosevelt offered a government ". . . bent on browbeating free enterprise and regimenting personal initiative. . . . Many youths have been kept on the dole, because the government persisted in shackling business and free enterprise. . . . In some respects, we think the New Dealers do not know their own minds. While they mean good, they do harm. . . ."

What was the point of fiddling with the great institutions and traditions of a system that had floated their forebears (and now, them) so surely, buoyantly, to the shores of well-being? No, the Andover man was preparing to serve those institutions, to stand at the helm for another generation, lest the great ship lose its way! In fact, the icon of Andover Hill was not the bald and befuddled academic, Dr. Feuss . . . but instead, the chairman of the academy's board, Henry L. Stimson. Now *there* was a life for the Andover man: Secretary of War under President Taft, Battalion Commander of Artillery during the Great War, Wall Street lawyer in the twenties, Governor General in the Philippines under Coolidge, Secretary of State to Hoover, and then, despite lifelong loyalty to the Republican Party, Secretary of War again in the Cabinet of FDR. . . . Stimson was, said the student who introduced him for a speech to Poppy and his classmates, "a living and vital representative of our ways and of our type of existence, who is out setting an example to the whole nation . . . living proof that the Andover Way is the way of men who guide the fortunes of nations."

What a bracing prospect was the rest of life, surveyed from the crest of Andover Hill! It was a glad and glorious path that led away from Phillips Hall, first to Yale (where P.A.'s best and brightest went to college), and thence to the boardrooms, the corridors of power, the Cabinet table.

Of course, their place at the helm was *not a birthright*— Andover was Not Like That. It was by merit that the Andover Man belonged. But what a Great and Good stroke of fortune for Poppy Bush: the Andover Way required of a man precisely the qualities he brought from home!

"The basic Andover code," said the student *Phillipian*, "assumes every student is first and foremost a gentleman." Honesty, loyalty, generosity, sportsmanship, and throughout, a becoming modesty (a bulwark for the years of triumph to come) . . . these were the qualities one needed, to belong.

He was only thirteen when he arrived, and had to struggle at first to fit in with his classmates, who were all at least a year older. (When Pressie had gone off to school at age five, little Poppy couldn't stand being alone in the house, so he'd started at Greenwich Country Day a year early.) He was still awfully small, in the fall of '37, and hardly seemed marked for stardom—not at all.

But then, strangely, a great stroke of fortune: in his third year at P.A., Poppy got sick, an infection in his shoulder that threatened to spread. There were no antibiotics at the time. Pres and

Dottie were worried half to death. It took a month, with the best of care at Massachusetts General, the finest hospital in the country, and then some specialists in New York, before all the doctors were sure that the boy would recover without ill effect.

The upshot was that Poppy repeated his third year at Andover, in the fall of '40. And when he came back, of course, he'd done all the schoolwork before, and that gave him more time for sports, where he showed what a year of growth and health could do for a young man, and where he was just as big as any boy, and felt himself, in fact, older and more mature than they, having been, in a sense, through all this before, and so, better able to help them out, to lead, as captain of the junior teams, on which he starred and swelled anew in the increasing approbation of his classmates and the older fellows, who noticed for the first time: here was a fellow who could play the game, and play it well! . . . And, of course, that meant he was tapped for the best club, and then as president of the Greeks, and then elected to the student council, and secretary of the student council, and treasurer of the student council, and then a student deacon. Society of Inquiry president, editorial board of the *Phillipian*, business board of the yearbook, Tea Dance committee, Senior Prom committee, president of the senior class . . . and captain of the soccer team, captain of the baseball team, and manager of the basketball team (until the coach saw him shoot one day and made him suit up as a player). . . . He became, in the Andover man's argot, an all-rounder. Wasn't it great how it worked out?

But the best thing was, he always watched out for the other guy, the younger men, the weaker ones. The great thing about

Poppy, other fellows at school used to say, was that *a fellow like him* would still talk to everybody, just as friendly to the juniors and lower-middles as he was to the grandest senior. In fact, he could drive you nuts: when the basketball coach told him he ought to suit up and play, Poppy said, "Oh, I couldn't do that! The other fellows worked hard to make the team! . . ." Finally, the coach, Frank DiClemente, had to tell him to shut up and put on his gym clothes. It was that, or wring his noble little neck. . . . But the point was, Poppy never sought his honors: he never had to, he had so many friends. And that *was* the Andover Way. One time, the *Phillipian* polled the students: "Do you think studies, friendships, or athletics are the most important in the long run?" Seventy-eight percent chose friendships. "The average student," the newspaper concluded, "came to Andover with making contacts uppermost in his mind."

It was the surest mark of his stardom that he never had to be out for himself. It was bad form to be out for oneself. Andover men not only wore the Blue like the fellows at Yale, there was an ethic they had in common, too: they were for God, Country, and Old Blue. An Andover man had to put something larger ahead of himself. Of course, Poppy was sound on that.

That was at the root of the excitement, as the war in Europe filled the papers, during their last two years, and it began to look like the men of '42 would have their chance to act in the world's highest drama: a war to rival their dads' Great War, a world for them to remake thereafter; this time, perhaps, more in their image. Clearly, Stimson heard the call to duty in 1940, when he took the post as War Secretary. (The word on campus was that Stimson was for U.S. entry, but FDR, as usual, dithered in politics.) If the U.S. did get in "over there," no one on Andover Hill doubted these young men would be called to lead. What a chance! To serve, to prove their mettle, to lead as they'd been raised to do, to command! Stimson came to speak to the seniors that year, 1940, while the Battle of Britain crackled from the radio every night. Certainly the world faced dark days, the great man said.

"But as I look into your faces and realize your responsibilities, I am filled, not with pity for you in what you are facing, but with a desire to congratulate you on your great opportunity.

"I envy you that opportunity.

"I would to God that I were young enough to face it with you."

All at once, the alumni news was filled with pictures of dashing young men in helmets, goggles, leather jackets: flying was just the thing, the only single combat in mechanized war, the knighthood of the modern service. The Andover men were leaving Yale, crossing the border, to sign up in Canada with the Royal Air Force. How could an Andover man stand idly by?

And, then, just on that glorious autumn day when Andover beat Exeter (by one point!) to finish an undefeated football season, the Japanese fleet sailed for Pearl Harbor. And two weeks later, just as Poppy was thrashing George "Red Dog" Warren in a long, do-or-die Ping-Pong match at AUV (the top club at school), the Japanese struck Pearl, the news spread in minutes, and Poppy and Red Dog put down their paddles and hurried back to the dorm. It was the same path they trod every day, from

AUV, past the Cochran Chapel . . . but now, everything was different. The air was electric. They were at war! . . .

"We stand," trumpeted the *Phillipian*, "as a unit against the common foe . . . the yellow peril of Nippon."

But all at once, their elders got cold feet! The young men of Andover Hill were told right away: they must stay in school! Dr. Feuss tried to keep P.A. calm, and bent to its business. At a special assembly, the following day, he told the men they must not run off to war, but let the draft fill the ranks, according to need and scientific methods. Pres Bush wrote to Poppy the same day: he ought to stay in school, go on to Yale. There'd be time after that to serve the flag.

But they were at war! This was his chance! Sure, Poppy would ask his coaches and teachers what they thought, but this was a personal thing, a matter of the code. The point was to know your own mind! If anyone doubted what Poppy would do, they had only to watch him on stage at that assembly, December 8, the morning after . . .

At ten o'clock, the whole school gathered in George Washington Hall, and Poppy was up front as senior class president. And when "The Star-Spangled Banner" started, the men were still slouching in front of their seats, as they always did in assembly. "Your country's at war!" said Dr. Feuss. "I expect when 'The Star-Spangled Banner' is played, I expect everyone here to be at attention!" But still there were a few wise guys who didn't know their world had changed. They were dicking around in the back! Poking each other and laughing, like they always had! And up on stage, Poppy Bush was burning! They were mocking the flag!

They were mocking Dr. Feuss! The bald doctor was standing there, helpless and frail, while they ignored him! *While we're at war!* Poppy Bush took a small step forward, and stared them down. He glared at them so hard, so visibly, that soon he had their gaze on him. And from the stage, in front of the men, likely for the first time in his life, Poppy Bush curled his upper lip in an ugly sneer of contempt.

By the time Christmas break rolled around, and he went to a dance, back home in Greenwich, where he met an auburn-haired beauty, Barbara Pierce, sixteen years old (and so eager to know him!), he didn't even mention staying in school. They sat out a waltz (Poppy never could waltz), and then sat out the next dance, and the next. But in all that talk, there was no confusion about what he was going to do. He was going to war. All the best fellows were. He would turn eighteen on Commencement Day, just a week after The Game (baseball with Exeter!) . . . and that was the big day. Poppy was going to sign up to fly. The Navy had a program that would get him his wings in less than a year. Gold Navy Wings! The knighthood!

On that day, Stimson arrived once again, in his bulletproof car, to address the school: the war would be long, the Secretary said. In good time, they would be called upon to lead, to rescue the right, to remake the world. But they would serve their country better by going on to college and getting as much education as they could, before they donned the uniform.

Wait, Stimson said, and let the draft do its work.

After the speech, Pres Bush met Poppy in the hallway outside the auditorium. Pres didn't have to bend down now to look straight into his son's eyes. "Well, George," he said in his big bass voice, "did the Secretary say anything to change your mind?"

"No, sir," Poppy said. "I'm going in."

Pres nodded, then shook his son's hand.

***

THIS WAS WHERE IT ended? The promise, the service, great doings to come, ended here in a world of green water, blue mist, alone, small . . . *this is it?* What was all that for, all the doing, trying, dear God, the blessed . . . *life*, what was that for? . . . But he kept searching the edge of his world, the hazy divide between air . . . green water . . . for the grand, bulking, blooming island of steel with the Stars and Stripes—all the guys! They had to come back! God, where were they . . . where were they where were they where were they . . .

Have to keep going, keep away, paddle, slap, pull, paddle, nothing out here, nothing but water, no water, no water, haze and water, blue and green, a speck over there, spots, bright bursting spots, and a speck, maybe it's a ship! No, not a ship, too small, not growing, yes growing, too small, not a ship, not the guys, slap to where, my hand! What's that thing it's taller, yes it's taller! It's taller, dear God, it's there yes what? Not a ship! Can't be a ship, just a speck, black dot, is this how it ends, seeing spots? God, God it's growing. A SUB! A SUB! A PERISCOPE DID THEY SEE ME GOD DID THEY SEE ME OVER HERE! OVER HERE HEY HERE HEY HERE I AM HERE ME HERE HEYYYY!

The conning tower rose from the water, and Bush, dazed,

bobbing, saw the hatch open and there was a man. *Jesus, what if it's Japs?* . . . There was something on his face. He had something up to his face. Something black. A beard! He had a beard! *NO JAPS WITH BEARDS!* A bearded seaman was holding something up, as Bush slapped and tore at the water toward the sub. A U.S. submarine, in three thousand miles of ocean, here was a U.S. submarine, come to get him! Dear God, come for HIM!

They got him, sailors on the deck now, the shape of the sub on the water, they pulled his raft, grabbed for him, pulled him up on shaky legs onto the steel deck, sweet Jesus, steel! And the seaman he saw was standing there, watching with this thing up to his face, a camera, a movie camera. They were filming. Three thousand godforsaken miles of ocean. They came to get him. They pulled him out. And they filmed it.

He'd been on the raft two hours.

"Welcome aboard, sir . . ."

The steel stairs poked up crazily at his legs as they half hauled him, half lowered him into a world of dark red light and overused air, clanking steel and the smell of men. The hatch closed. They were getting out, getting the hell out of there.

"Welcome aboard, sir . . ."

They stretched him out flat, swabbed his head. He'd be all right, he heard them say. The guys on the *Finback* always liked this, this pilot rescue duty, when they fished them out and watched them wake up to a new world below the sea. . . . What would the guy say?

"Welcome aboard the *Finback*, sir . . ."

But as the guys on the *Finback* remembered it, Bush was

distraught, kept asking for his crew, half-delirious. . . . Then, no words, just tears.

HE WAS ON THE sub for a month, while it hunted the Pacific for Japanese ships, and when the *Finback* dropped him off at Midway, he likely could have fiddled a ticket home. The Navy didn't want shaky pilots, men with second thoughts. But Bush hitched a ride west across the ocean, and then another to his ship, back to the guys. Of course, they greeted him like a lost brother:

"George Herbert Walker Bush!"

No one asked much about the day he was shot down. They knew how it was: he'd lost two friends.

There were a half-dozen more missions in the Philippines, but VT-51's number was up. By December, they were steaming home. Bush got to Greenwich on Christmas Eve. Poppy made it back! After that horrible telegram, saying he was shot down! He was *here*! Christmas Eve! Everyone was crying, laughing, hugging. He looked great! He was home! It was like a movie!

And then, after New Year's, in his snappy dress blues, he married his dark-haired sweetheart, Barbara Pierce. What was the point of dawdling? It could all end in a puff of smoke—just like *that*. There was a honeymoon, just a few days, on Sea Island, off the Georgia coast, and then a new posting to Virginia Beach. Of course, he'd have to go back to the war. They were only halfway to Tokyo. He'd get another squadron, and Bar would go back to college, to Smith. . . . But then, Truman dropped the bomb, and they got the news: the Nips had folded! No invasion! No more war! It was over! The Blessed Confluence!

Poppy was out of the Navy in a month, off to Yale the same September. What was the point of dawdling? Three years of his life were gone. There was a child on the way. There sure wasn't time to moon about the war, to talk about the day the plane went down, Delaney and White (never did know what happened to them), or the way they came to get him, Lieutenant George Herbert Walker Bush, out of thousands of miles of ocean. He had the Air Medal and two Gold Stars, and then the Distinguished Flying Cross: he was a hero, but he wasn't going to bring that up. He'd done his part. That was all he'd say.

He didn't even pick up any cheap points with Bar, saying he'd thought of her when he thought he was a goner, in the ocean. And she, being Bar, didn't ask if he did.

No one in his family could remember talking about it. Must have been dreadful, they agreed. And, being Walkers, and Bushes, they didn't bring it up.

It was only years later, when he got into politics and had to learn to retail bits of his life, that he ever tried to put words around the war.

His first attempts, in the sixties, were mostly about the *cahm-rah-deree* and the spirit of the American Fighting Man. The Vietnam War was an issue then, and Bush was for it. (Most people in Texas were.) He said he learned "a lot about life" from his years in the Navy—but he never said what the lessons were.

Later, when peace was in vogue, Bush said the war had "sobered" him with a grave understanding of the cost of conflict—

he'd seen his buddies die. The voters could count on him not to send their sons to war, because he knew what it was.

Still later, when he turned presidential prospect, and every bit of his life had to be melted down to the coin of the realm—character—Bush had to essay more thoughts about the war, what it meant to him, how it shaped his soul. But he made an awful hash of it, trying to be jaunty. He told the story of being shot down. Then he added: "Lemme tell ya, that'll make you start to think about the separation of church and state . . ."

Finally, in a much-edited transcript of an interview with a minister whom he hired as liaison to the born-again crowd, Bush worked out a statement on faith and the war: something sound, to cover the bases. It wasn't foxhole Christianity, and he couldn't say he saw Jesus on the water—no, it was quieter than that. . . . But there, on the *Finback*, he spent his time standing watch on deck in the wee hours, silent, reflective, under the bright stars . . .

"It was wonderful and energizing, a time to talk to God.

"One of the things I realized out there all alone was how much family meant to me. Having faced death and been given another chance to live, I could see just how important those values and principles were that my parents had instilled in me, and of course how much I loved Barbara, the girl I knew I would marry. . . ."

That was not quite how he was recalled by the men of the *Finback*. Oh, they liked him: a real funny guy. And they gave him another nickname, Ellie. That was short for Elephant. What they recollected was Bush in the wardroom, tossing his head and emitting on command the roaring trumpeted squeal of the enraged pachyderm; it was the most uncanny imitation of an elephant.

Nor were "sobered" or "reflective" words that leapt to Bar's mind when she remembered George at that time. The image she recalled was from their honeymoon, when she and George strolled the promenades, amid the elderly retirees who wintered at that Sea Island resort. All at once, George would scream "AIR RAID! AIR RAID!" and dive into the shrubs, while Bar stood alone and blushing on the path, prey to the pitying glances of the geezers who clucked about "that poor shell-shocked young man."

But there was, once, a time when he talked about the war, at night, at home, to one friend, between campaigns, when he didn't have to cover any bases at all.

"You know," he said, "it was the first time in my life I was ever scared.

"And then, when they came and pulled me out . . ." (Him, Dottie Bush's son, out of a million miles of empty ocean!)

"Well . . ." Bush trailed off, pleasantly, just shaking his head.

2

ADVENTURE WAS NOT A word that would have leapt to most minds in that apartment. Nothing wrong with Hillhouse Avenue, of course: the president of Yale lived next door. But 37 Hillhouse was cut up into thirteen flats, divvied out to married veterans with children. So thirteen couples lived in the house, each with a child, save for one couple with twins: that made forty souls altogether. And they were lucky to get the place. After the war, when almost ten million men and women suddenly qualified for the GI Bill, the campuses took the brunt of the avalanche. The vets lived in trailers, Quonset huts, abandoned barracks. At the University of California, couples were living in cars.

Poppy and Bar were extra-lucky: they had their own bathroom. The two couples with whom they shared a kitchen also had to share a bathroom. That was apparently too much to take. So the two other couples feuded endlessly, and there were battles about the two refrigerators that three couples (and three children) had to share. One of the neighbors got so furious at the others that he brought in inspectors to test their germs. He claimed there were more germs in their fridge than in the sewers of New Haven. Mostly, the other couples never spoke. One family ate at five and the other at seven, so they wouldn't have to pass. Well, utopia this was not.

But adventure . . . it surely was, to Barbara Bush. New Haven was the first place Bar had lived on her own, without her parents, or some school authority (or the U.S. Navy, which greeted her as a bride) ruling her destiny *in loco parentis.*

Ever since Bar could remember, her mother and older sister had imposed their wisdom on whatever Bar had to do. Her mother, Pauline Pierce, another daughter of the good Midwest (her father, James Robinson, served on Ohio's first Supreme Court), was a woman of great and refined beauty, an insatiable, somewhat spendthrift collector of beautiful things, and a woman of expert enthusiasms. Horticulture, fine needlepoint, management of the home and children, matters of dress, taste, and decorum—Pauline had firm, often idiosyncratic, ideas on *everything,* and her notions, however insupportable, were not subject to argument. She was a joiner and a ferocious doer, who had, as Barbara concluded at length, not much sense of humor in general, and none about herself or her children. Barbara's older sister, Martha, got her mother's looks, her brains, and her temperament: she had definite ideas, five years' more experience on the planet, and no discernible shyness about instructing her ungainly younger sister. What's more, Martha was thin. Barbara was not.

Barbara was what parents call a big-boned girl: at age

twelve, she stood five-foot-eight and weighed, as she would forever recall, one hundred forty-eight pounds. Pauline had definite
ideas on food, and the Pierces sat to a splendid table: garden
vegetables shining with butter, mashed potatoes, real cream for
the cereal. . . . Pauline would urge: "Eat up, Martha . . . *Not you,
Barbara* . . ." It was maddening: Martha stayed thin, no matter
what. Barbara might have taken the contrast more to heart were
it not for her father (whose big bones, after all, she'd inherited)
defending his favorite.

Marvin Pierce was a big, broad-faced man, easygoing, funny,
a splendid athlete at Miami of Ohio, yet another scion of good
Midwest manufacturers who'd moved the family east to New
York, and thence to the stately commuter town of Rye, New
York, as he climbed the ladder at McCall Publishing. By the time
his third child, Barbara, was born, Marvin had long since learned
to survive his wife's fierce certainties with resort to irreverent
humor and the quiet pleasures of the golf course.

Barbara learned to survive, too, with her own mix of ir-
reverence and imagination. She was a great reader, not only of
the classic girls' books of the day, *Little Women*, *Jane Eyre*, and
the dog stories by Albert Payson Terhune, but also the serial
stories that appeared in her father's McCall company maga-
zines. Then, too, there were McCall pattern books, suitable for
Barbara and her friends to cut up, to dress a thousand paper
dolls, for romance and daring exploit in all corners of the world.
There was her dog, Sandy, to run with, her bike to ride through
the neighborhood, tree-climbing, rope-skipping, swimming in
Long Island Sound, tennis lessons (Barbara had her father's—

ungirlish, at the time—love of sport), and a general unconcern for dainty appearance. Even after she'd slimmed down to quite a lovely young woman herself; even after she'd followed Martha's path, and Pauline's notion of proper education, to three years at a finishing school (Ashley Hall) in South Carolina; even after she'd followed Martha, again, to Smith College (where Martha had been discovered by *Vogue* and photographed for its cover as "College Girl of the Year"); even after Christmas '41, when her large bright eyes and open smile, her off-the-shoulder green-and-red dress, her flowing auburn hair and soft, pale skin had attracted the notice of Poppy Bush across the dance floor at the Round Hill Club in Greenwich, Connecticut, Barbara Pierce was a young woman notable for not putting all her stock in appearance. Identity (hers, at least) was distinct from pose. She was, fetchingly, Not That Way. In fact, as Poppy was amazed to discover, as they sat out a dance, then a second, and a third, she was better at spotting airs or airheads, better at eschewing pretense, more direct, more down-to-earth, than he! And why not? Poppy was Not That Way as an act of civility. But Bar was a natural: hers was an act of survival.

As for her, she thought he was, well . . . wonderful. Attractive, accomplished at school, funny . . . he wasn't stuck-up like some big seventeen-year-olds could be . . . he was just . . . perfect! Bar would later tell her children that she married the first man she ever kissed. (It always made them retch when she said it.) Later still, when she was campaigning, and her life was laid out for viewing on a hundred hotel coffee tables, she was always asked: *How did you know he was The One?* Well, she'd say, it was simple: "Whenever he came into a room, I had a hard time breathing."

But for the moment, for a long time, there was still the family. . . . Right after that fateful Christmas dance, Barbara came back from the Round Hill Club and mentioned she'd met a nice boy, Poppy Bush. That was at two A.M. By the time Barbara awoke the following day, Pauline had been on the phone all morning, finding out *everything* about the family. (Thank heaven, all reports were good.) Even after matters had progressed for two years, and Poppy and Bar were adult enough to plan a marriage, there was still a supply of female family wisdom:

"Now Barbara, you'll have to pick out silver, and you must get the most ornamental pattern you can find. Take it from me, dear, it's so much easier to clean . . ." So Bar scoured the stores for the plainest, flattest silver made. It was time to get out from under.

For a while, marriage only stepped up the family pressure. Greenwich and Rye were ten miles apart, and now, of course, they were in constant communication. At Christmas, and like family conclaves, Poppy and Bar would drive back and forth for breakfast at one house, lunch at another, a stop with the uncles (Poppy didn't like to disappoint), eggnog here and supper there . . . like Ping-Pong balls in a closed room! One day, when she was very pregnant with Georgie, and visiting in Greenwich with Pres and Dottie, Bar hauled herself out of a chair, and announced she had to visit in Rye, her parents . . . she was expected. . . . Pres Bush said sternly, but just as a joke: "Did we give you permission to visit those strangers?" It was no joke to Bar. She dissolved in tears.

SHE NEVER REALLY SAID to Pop: "Let's get out . . ." She didn't have to. That was one of the great things about him, about them together. There was so much they just knew . . . and from the beginning. Sometimes, people asked her: How did Poppy propose? Well, he didn't. They just started planning. Of course, she didn't propose children either. She just took care of it.

She knew Poppy was as eager as she to get out on his own. Maybe more: he'd been to war, he'd seen the world. Now he was hustling through Yale in two and a half years, but he wasn't just going to scrape through. With his straight A's in economics, letters in soccer and baseball, as the last man tapped for Skull and Bones—only fifteen chosen, the best of the best—he could have been a lock for a Rhodes scholarship, an extra year of study at a university in England. But what was the point? George Bush wasn't interested in more theory. Anyway, a family of three would never make it through a year on the stipend. Poppy would have to ask his folks for money—that's another thing he wanted to get past. He wanted to be out on his own—Bar and he even talked about farming, the most self-sufficient family life . . . but after they found out how much it would cost for land, seed, stock, equipment . . . well, Poppy wasn't going to ask Pres for that kind of dough. No way!

So, it was business. That's where the action was, anyway. With the rationing lifted and factories switching to production of cars, washers, fridges, *televisions*! . . . things were on the move . . . fortunes being made. The wave of strikes that followed the war was mostly over now, and the engine of U.S. business was never going to sink back to the sleepy sputter of the thirties. If the theories in his economics class meant anything, that was the lesson: America owned the world's markets as no other nation had before. (If the government would get its hands off the levers, there was no telling how fast, how far, the great ship of progress could sail!) American business won the war, and now it *ruled* this brave new world. And here was Poppy Bush, bred to captaincy, just itching to work his way to the helm. Wasn't it great how it turned out?

But he had to start somewhere, and fast. He was a senior already! Procter & Gamble had a trainee program, he talked to their recruiters, but . . . no soap. Lots of fellows were going into banking, or stocks, pure business, the capitalism of capital. And that would have been easy for Pop. Gampy Walker had split away from the Harrimans and formed his own investment bank, G. H. Walker & Co. His son, Herbie, was running the company now. He would have leapt to take Poppy on. For that matter, there were whispers that Brown Brothers Harriman might even bend its own strict rule on nepotism . . . Pres Bush's son was a star!

But that wasn't the way: not for Poppy. If he'd wanted to play it safe and sound, he never would have signed up to fly on his eighteenth birthday: could have started Yale five years ago. Where was the adventure in that?

In the stiff-upper-lip world of the Walkers, no one tried to *talk* to Poppy about his choices: certainly not! . . . Unless he asked, which he wouldn't. Of course, they'd do anything for him: they were so eager, it was almost uncomfortable. When Poppy and Bar would show up in Maine, it was like the prodigal son had returned: Kill the Fatted Calf! Uncle Herbie—the second G. H. Walker, and the second patriarch of the Point—just *adored* Poppy, idolized him. George Bush could do no wrong: George was a winner, a star at school, a hero in war, a pilot—the knighthood! Herbie's dream was to fly with Poppy. Of course, Herbie didn't know a thing about flying. He was scared to death of thunder and lightning! But he learned to fly at the close of the war, and went out to Detroit and *bought an airplane*. But then he started to fly it back East, and hit a snowstorm and couldn't go on; couldn't get back to Detroit, either. So, in the end, he landed his new plane in a cornfield and just walked away. That was the end of Herbie the Pilot.

But it didn't cool Herbie's ardor, not at all. Whenever he'd hear Pop and Bar were coming up to Maine, Herbie dropped *everything* in a frenzy of setting up golf games, tennis matches, picnics, dinner parties. He started a whole summer baseball league . . . Poppy's coming! Everyone thought it was awful for Herbie's own sons, Bert and Ray. Herbie was so obviously in love with their cousin. Poppy didn't quite know what to do about it. He always tried to be extra-nice to Bert and Ray.

It was just another thing that would be . . . easier, once Poppy and Bar got away on their own. As for going into business with Herbie, in his firm, well . . . that didn't seem like a good idea.

Pres's great friend (and fellow Bonesman) Neil Mallon, in Cleveland, had been unofficial godfather to the Bush kids. He knew Poppy was hunting a place to start on his own. So he talked to George about the Texas oil fields: that was the place for a young man to make his fortune. Mallon was the head of Dresser Industries (Pres Bush served on the board, of course), and Dresser owned Ideco, an oil-field equipment company. Why didn't George go out there as a trainee, learn the oil business from the ground up? Mallon didn't have to say the rest: he didn't have any kids of his own. . . . If Poppy liked what he saw of Ideco, and Dresser, well . . . there'd be opportunities.

Poppy liked what he heard. He'd been posted to Texas in the Navy for a couple of months. It was wide open . . . a whole new world . . . a thousand miles away. And everything about Texas oil had the air of great doings, men and fortunes larger than life. Like everyone else of his generation, Bush had seen the stories in *Life* magazine, the *Fortune* profiles of H. L. Hunt, Clint Murchison, Sid Richardson, Eamon Carter. They were Giants in a Giant Land. . . . Oil! Black Gold! . . . What an adventure!

So Poppy came back from his talk with Neil Mallon and said to Bar, he thought he'd get a job with Ideco, the International Derrick and Equipment Company. It was the oil business! . . . A trainee's job . . . *lots* of opportunity . . . starting wage just over three hundred dollars a month.

It sounded good to Bar. Reasonably stable. And she knew Pop would do well, wherever he chose to work . . . and if it didn't turn out, well, they'd find another way. Pop was Phi Beta Kappa at Yale, after all. It's not like they were going to another country . . . were they? . . . Where is this?

"Odessa, Texas," he said.

Bar paused a couple of beats and then favored Poppy with a radiant smile. "I've *always wanted*," she said, "to live in Odessa, Texas."

In June, after the College World Series and Graduation Day in New Haven, Poppy packed up his new red Studebaker (a graduation gift from Pres), and started driving south. Bar and Georgie went up to Walker's Point, to wait for Pop to find them a home. It was just a few days before they got the letter with the good news: Poppy was a star! Of course, all his Yale training was wrong, but he was getting better with a broom, and the boss said he was the best warehouse sweeper that Ideco's Odessa Branch Office ever had.

And he'd found them a house—well, half a house. (He wrote that it was "kind of humble.") So Bar and Georgie got an airplane to Dallas and then to the Midland-Odessa field, a propeller-flight journey of more than twelve hours, to join George in their strange new world . . . and my, wasn't it exotic!

First, it was flat, perfectly flat, like no land they'd ever seen. No brooks, streams, rivers. No native trees—no trees. It was bright, and hot like they'd never felt heat, and gritty everywhere with dust. The blacktop into town from the airport shimmered between opposing ranks of strange, hulking drill rigs, piles of steel pipe, casing, tubing, decking, cable . . . all baked in the sun-grit, like ossified armies standing guard on the tatty tin or cinder-block sheds housing the businesses behind. And then, as George and Bar turned onto their street, East Seventh, the pavement gave way altogether, and they rolled on two ruts of dust to a stop, in front of their new home.

It was a shotgun house—tiny in the first place, but now partitioned down the middle, so two families could each have a narrow half-living room, just inside the concrete front step, and then a counter giving on to a tiny kitchen, and one narrow bedroom in the rear. The partition ended at the back, with the bathroom, which both tenants shared. It was one of the few bathrooms on the street. Most had an outhouse in the boxy backyard, like Mr. Wagley, two doors down, whose outhouse shared his rear plot of dust with the junk he collected for a living, and his wagon, and his horse. The immediate neighbors, in the other half of the shotgun house, were a mother and her daughter (and the daughter's toddler daughter), who made their living entertaining male guests, which pretty much tied up the bathroom, from sundown on.

It was all so . . . interesting! You just didn't *see* stuff like that in Rye, or Greenwich—even New Haven. In fact, back in Rye, Pauline Pierce thought poor Barbara must be desperate: *Odessa!* It smacked of Russia and want. She kept sending cold cream, and boxes of soap flakes, convinced that privation dogged her daughter at that edge of the earth. But there was no privation, no desperation. In fact, it was only thirty-five years later, when George Bush had to convince the world that he wasn't some timid toy poodle, that it ever came to be described as a roll of the dice, a gamble. . . . At the time, it was just *a wonderful adventure!* See, it *wasn't* really their world. George and Bar always knew that—they weren't trapped. They could always go back . . . or go somewhere else. They were in it, and yet, not quite of it, immune to enjoy it like expatriates who talk with fascination about "the locals" and their strange folkways.

Such *fun:* high school football on Friday nights, with a crowd twice as big as Yale ever drew, all in their shirtsleeves, fanning themselves in the twilight heat, and girl cheerleaders! Never saw *that* back East! . . . And barbecues over a fire in an oil drum, and grits, and chili, and chicken-fried steak at Agnes' Café. *Oh, we love that stuff!* . . . And the strange and humorous things that George would report when he came home, about the squinty stares he drew at the oil field, or out painting pumps, with the good ol' bubbas in the heat and the grit . . .

Boy. Jus' whu'the hayl 'r yew dooin' out 'ere ennuhways?

The short answer was: living high and free, on three hundred seventy-five dollars a month. And learning, sometimes the hard way. . . . A couple of days after they moved onto Seventh Street, Bar woke them all up in the middle of the night. Gas! She smelled it . . .

Get out!

Get Georgie!

GET OUT!

DON'T LIGHT A MATCH!

Thing was, there were always a couple hundred wells flaring off within the city limits, a refinery, a few hundred tanks. . . . Odessa, as the wakened neighbors pointed out, always kinda smelled like that . . . ma'am.

THE BIG EXCITEMENT THAT fall was the Jugoslav who came to visit, to study American oil operations. The head office of Dresser sent him down, with carte blanche. But that didn't mean the good ol' bubbas wanted foreigners—a commie!—snoopin' around. So the eager Jugo gentleman got kicked down the ladder and landed in the lap of . . . George Bush.

What fun! It went on for days and days. George and Bar

took the guy all over West Texas. Took him for barbecue. Took him to a football game. The fellow had his notebook, with everything he wanted to learn, and anytime a fact penetrated the language haze, he'd write this, too, in his book. The big thing he wanted was . . . *skiddarig*. That was a shortcut they'd figured out in West Texas. If a hole was dry or played out, and the drilling equipment was needed elsewhere, they wouldn't have to take down the rig: they'd move it whole, *skid* it, sometimes hundreds of yards down the field, to the next location. Well, that was the cat's pyjamas at the Ministry in Belgrade, in '48. *"Skiddarig?"* the Jugoslav implored. So George Bush, whose highest attainment in the oil business, to that point, was a clerkship in an equipment warehouse, learned how to skid a rig . . . and how to explain it without benefit of words.

Words weren't Bush's strong suit, anyway. There was something extraverbal about his friendliness, his eagerness, the way his smile bent his whole body toward the guy, or the light, friendly bubba punch to the shoulder to show he was making a joke, the way Bush flung his legs out when he sank into a chair at home, told the Jugoslav that *he* could feel at home there, too. It was an animal thing . . . the same bodily aw-shucks with which Bush let Texans know they needn't mind his back-East college-boy talk.

How could they mind, when he was so happy to get to know them, to make their home his, to have them think well of him? Hell, here he was, after a few months, West Texas's own ambassador to the foreigners. Thing was, he was so . . . accepting. Here was a fellow who came from outside, but he didn't act like it . . .

didn't judge them like a stranger. Wasn't that way. The way they saw it, the way they said it, Bush was just a hell of a good guy, tried to fit in, played the game.

As for him and Bar, they'd decided: they *loved* West Texas. The way people took you in! . . . You couldn't find nicer folks, no matter where you went. . . . Late that fall, they decided they weren't even going home for Christmas. Of course, they'd miss everybody back East: they sent out, must have been a *hundred* Christmas cards . . . but it was just too long a trip with a two-year-old in tow. And they had their own life to live now, even for the holidays. So they made their own preparations in their half a house, and they did their shopping and found a tree, and everything was ready by Christmas Eve. . . .

Ideco had a party that afternoon—a West Texas custom, Bush figured—and customers and friends dropped in, and George helped out, mixing drinks. And he wanted to fit in and be friendly, of course, so as they hoisted each glass he poured, he'd hoist one, too . . . and he did fine until a whole 'nother set of guests trooped in, a second shift to the office party . . . but he poured more drinks and, just to be friendly . . . It got to be dark, and well past dark, and Bar was still waiting with the dinner at home, and the tree was there, undecorated, and it got quite late, and George was being friendly, fitting right in, on his own now, and . . . Anyway, they brought him home in the bed of the company pickup, rolled him gently out onto his lawn, and that Christmas Eve he was truly on his own, though he didn't know much about it, shit-faced, on his back, under the stars, in Odessa, Texas.

3

~~~THEY CALLED IT THE independent oil business, and that was one of the lures for George Bush: it even sounded right. He liked the strange, fierce language of this last American frontier, the barren Texas plain: the land men, promoting a deal, to carve out an override . . . buying mineral, or royalty, at The Spot, over a bowl of red . . . grabbing off a farm-out from a major, or wild-catting a field where there was show, but they plugged and called her a duster. . . .

It was the only foreign language George Bush ever took to. But, for him, its highest incarnation was the honorable title borne by all the young go-getters: *independents* . . . now, that was something to be. That's what he was out here for, and it worked: he won his independence. It wasn't till he'd been a Texan for years, and was an oilman himself, shopping around for investors one day, that anybody thought to introduce him as "Pres Bush's boy. . . ." It sounded so strange, by that time, struck him so odd, that he went home and told Bar about it: first time in *years* he'd heard that.

But, of course, there was more than the name: there were all the truths it implied. It was a perfect business for George Bush—he had everything it took. The first fact was, the business rested entirely on personal relations. The goal of the independent was to put himself in the middle of deals. That meant finding out where deals were being done. You could find out some from the maps, where a dot marked each oil well, and you could find out more from the county land records, which showed who was buying land, or leasing mineral rights, in which tracts, and for how much. But once a deal hit the maps or the courthouse, it was done. What you wanted were deals in the making, the newest geology, the plans of the majors . . . and for that, well, you had to chat up the geologists for the majors, and their scouts, and the ranchers around the countryside, the abstractors around the county courthouse, and your fellow independents . . . you had to ply them, wine and dine them, ask about their kids, be sure to say hey in church. . . . In short, you made friends. And no one would have more friends than George Bush. Once a deal was in the works, it was all done on handshakes—there were no lawyers around a table. Hell, lots of times, there was no table! Your word and your good name were your primary business assets: you had to play by the rules, the code. And no one was more sensitive to the code than Bush. It was like school, but better: the rewards weren't grades, or honors, but cash.

In fact, it was like an eastern boys' school, in those days, in Midland, Texas. Many of the young independents came from back East, from Ivy League schools. The locals called them "the Yalies." Actually, they weren't all Elis. Toby Hilliard and his partner, John Ashmun, were from Princeton, as was

47

Pomeroy Smith—class of '46, was Pom. There was a Princeton Club in Midland, with thirteen members. . . . And the Liedtke brothers, Hugh and Bill, were Oklahoma boys, from an established oil family in Tulsa, but they came out of Amherst and Dartmouth. . . . Earle Craig, like Bush, was from Yale. There was an ad hoc Yale Club in Midland, too. And, of course, a Harvard Club—there were dozens of these bright, young Yankees around. They were the best and the bravest of the Ivy League, the boys who weren't going to sit in some office, after they'd seen the world in the war. And smart—they were all smart, it went without saying—but that was another thing about this business: it was better to be lucky than smart. It didn't matter what you knew, or even whom. You could have all the geology on a formation, and production figures from working wells five hundred feet away on every side, and you'd put a hole smack in the middle . . . and nothin', not a drop, a duster. Go figure. . . . So, no matter what else he did, an independent had to roll the dice. At a certain point, you had to trust to your luck. And no one was luckier than Bush.

The third thing about the business had to do with the same hard, dusty fact: everyone bored some dry holes. So, the trick was to drill a *lot* of holes. If you were in one deal, it was make or break; but if you were in forty deals, you'd get production *somewhere.* The essence of the business was activity: new friends, new deals, a sixteenth of an interest here, an eighth there, maybe three thirty-seconds, and you'd carry the friend who got you into it for the drilling costs, down to the casing point. . . . The deals were anything the market would bear: whatever you could get a handshake on. Most of the independents didn't have the capital to act like majors: simply lease the mineral rights under a piece of land, drill the wells, and sell the oil. Instead, they had to do a lot of little deals: maybe leasing mineral rights from a rancher, then running, that very afternoon, to the office of a major to sell that lease for five percent more. Or they'd take on a drilling contractor as a partner, and keep a share of the production, if a well on that lease hit. But even for the littlest players, it was the same game: in general, the business would reward hyperkinesis. And George Bush never could sit still.

In fact, none of those boys could: it was go-go-go, every day during the boom years—and most of the nights. By seven or eight in the morning, you'd see the Yalies hustling up Wall Street (for a long time, the only paved street in town), to The Spot, which was the coffee shop in the Midland Tower, or to Agnes' Café, or the Scharbauer Hotel, with the flush of a big-deal-to-come on their cheeks, and maps under their arms, ready to unfurl on the first table they saw, after which their finger would trace the line of that trap . . . right there, see? . . . while they explained that this thing was surefire! Just barely got in there ahead of those bastards at Texaco! . . . At night, while they sipped beer and barbecued in empty oil drums, they'd talk about one thing—oil—who was buying where, who was drilling, what kind of rock they hit at three thousand feet, and what royalty was fetching now on the west edge of Ector County. They'd dream and scheme and talk about the Big One . . . the one they all meant to hit, the one that would put them on the map. It only took one. That was the beauty of the game. At one party, when all the Yalies gathered (they always were together, it seemed), Toby Hilliard leaned back in a chair and mused to the crowd at large: "You know," said Toby, "some of us in this room are going to be *very, very* rich."

The thing with Bush, it wasn't just about wealth: sure, he wanted to get rich, like anyone else . . . but not private-island rich, Monte-Carlo-in-the-winter rich. What drew him, what he had to have, was the game itself, the great doings . . . so absorbing, so *do-or-die*. This was a game where he could shine!

It was from big Pres that Poppy, and all the Bush kids, took their attitude toward the game itself: the seriousness of playing well, the appreciation of form. Prescott Bush demanded much of himself, and he did not play a game to hack around. He had been a Yale first baseman, at six-foot-four, a towering slugger who'd hit the ball a mile—would have had twice as many homers if he could have run faster. Not only was Pres elected captain of the ball team, he'd occasionally succumb to entreaty from the golf team. *(Pres, we've got to have you, we've got Penn today!)* So he'd play against another school's best golfer in the morning, then suit up in Yale flannels for a one-thirty ball game. He was still a scratch golfer into his fifties, and never would accept the demands of a Wall Street partnership, or later, his duties as a U.S. Senator, as excuse for shoddy play. There was one way to ensure that you'd never be invited to play golf with Pres again, and that was to talk while he was putting.

Still, Pres mostly played against the golf course and his own human tendency to error. The competitive fire, the will to win, Poppy got from his mother's family, the Walkers. It was always sink or swim with the Walkers. The old man, the grandfather, G. H. Walker, was as hard a handful of business iron as the Midwest ever produced. It was he who transplanted the family from St. Louis to a mansion in New York, so he could play in capitalism's big leagues with the Vanderbilts and Harrimans. That was the same league he played as a sportsman. For a while, he kept a stable of racing horses in partnership with Averell Harriman. When his friend (and rival) in St. Louis, Dwight Davis, created the Davis Cup championship for tennis amateurs in Britain and the United States, Gampy Walker created the Walker Cup for the amateurs of golf. In his later years, he headed the New York State Racing Commission and served as president of the United States Golf Association.

But those were the public connections to sport. It was in private that he practiced and passed on the religion of games, chiefly in Kennebunkport, Maine, where, at the turn of the century, he bought seventeen acres of rocky coastline as the Walker clan's summer preserve. For the Walkers, the long days in Maine were a whirlwind of contests. There were boat races from the harbor to Walker's Point. (And not in the genteel, silent canoes or sailboats that other families kept; Pops Walker favored powerboats, big ones.) There were pickup ball games, in the family, at the Point itself, or bigger games on the town field for the summer league that Gampy Walker created, staffed with town boys and college players brought to Maine for the summer, so his own sons could have summer baseball experience. There were daily and twice-daily golf matches, and tennis matches, pitting parents and children, cousins and uncles, Walkers and friends, against one another in an ever-shifting, always ranked, round-robin to determine *the best*. In some ways, golf was the fiercest: it was his game. By the time his sons came of age and honed their skills enough to beat him, they'd also learned a dozen little ruses ("Oh, sorry, Father . . . Bill's counting on me for a foursome") to dodge the dread despair and *rage*, somewhere on the back nine, when the old man found himself four down, with only three to play. Even when younger, tennis-playing Walkers would hit the River Club, Court One (pretty much the only court they'd play on), everyone knew it: no other members were so energetic, noisy, clannish, and competitive. No other matches had the same air of seriousness, of importance, *do-or-die*. And when there was a championship, or like cataclysm, there would be G. H. Walker himself, attending in his very clean white-and-brown saddle shoes, tweed jacket and necktie, stiff white collar, white flannel trousers, and straw boater.

One summer, when son Louis and daughter Dorothy were a mixed-doubles team playing for the River Club's junior cup, G. H. Walker appeared at Court One, but Lou was nowhere to be seen. He claimed later he didn't know the match was on. It turned out he was at the bathing beach, fooling around and drinking with friends. So the old man had Lou summoned. And he showed up loaded, *snockered*, in front of the whole club! He tossed a ball for a serve and *whiffed*. He was *staggering* on the court. The old man departed, leaving word: he would see Louis, after the match . . . in his room. When Lou got back to the Point, much sobered (by match end, he hadn't played so badly), the old man didn't wait for explanation. He announced to Lou: "You're not going to college. You're too *stupid* to go to college. You're going to work." That same evening, Lou was packed, and on his way to a year in the coal mines in Bradford, Pennsylvania.

In time, all the Walker kids got the religion. But pound for pound, perhaps the best was Dottie, the younger of two daughters, the pearl in this pan of gravel. Not only was she bright and beautiful (they were all *so* attractive), but she seemed to have in her small form the distillate of the Walker ethic: she played to win. When Betty Trotter, a girlfriend at Kennebunkport, challenged Dottie to a swim from the River Club pier, all the Walker boys knew that Dottie wouldn't stop until Betty did. But when Betty quit, after twelve hundred yards in choppy open sea, Dottie just kept swimming, more than a mile, straight to Walker's Point. No one had to make allowances for Dottie in competition. When she married Prescott Bush, and had her own kids to raise, she served as the one-woman ranking committee: it was she who made the matches, pitting Bushes against Bushes, Bushes against Walkers, and Bushes against friends, in the constant contest to be the best.

And it wasn't just summers, not just in Maine: in their year-round home in Greenwich, Connecticut, the Bush kids played games constantly. If there wasn't a ball game at the Greenwich Country Day School, or a tennis match at the Field Club, they'd gather their friends for football at the Bush house, where there was room, and a ready welcome from Dottie. The house on Grove Lane was a magnet for kids: if it rained, all the friends might still show up, to play indoor football in the long upstairs hall, or Ping-Pong on the table in the front hall (Dottie finally tired of taking it down—that table was the first thing visitors saw), or some game that Poppy made up, on the spot. Poppy never liked to be alone. And he was so good about sharing, making sure everyone was included. For a while, Dottie and the housekeeper, Antonina, called him Have-half, because once, when he got a new wagon, he turned to a friend and offered: "Have half? . . ." Of course, he had the most little friends. When Pres would come home on the train from New York and find a house taken over by children at play, he'd sigh and inquire of his wife: "Dottie, do they all have to be here?" But even when Pres was home, and didn't want a bunch of wild Indians in the halls, Dottie would sneak the boys' friends up the back stairs so they could play. After supper, when Pres was closeted with important telephone calls, Dottie, daughter Nan, and all the boys were likely in the living room, locked in a vicious tiddlywinks match: so serious, involving, so *do-or-die*, that it wasn't uncommon for a child to leave the room in tears, after being "shot out."

Withal, Dottie brought something new to the religion: a certain refinement, a polish, the product of one more generation under the buffer of good society. In Dottie's house there was all the Walker competition, but none of the loudness about it. She did not abide bragging. Her boys were not to come crashing into the dining room, to announce: "I mopped up the court with Gerry." God forbid! They could not even announce: "I won." In the Bush household, young people were expected not only to win, but to be good winners. The proper way was to wait, to be asked:

"Didn't you have a match today?"

"Uh huh, with Gerry."

"Oh, lovely! How'd you do?"

And then, the proper answer was to offer some excuse for Gerry, avoiding the first-person pronoun altogether, or at most, to say, quietly: "I was lucky."

It was all right if a brother or sister did a bit of bragging for you: "Oh, Poppy was great! He had three hits . . ."

But if one of the Bush boys was asked about his game, and he blurted: "I had a home run!" Dottie's voice would take on a hint of edge: "That's lovely, dear. How'd the *team* do?" Sometimes, that edge could cut to the bone. When Poppy, age twelve, was asked about his tennis match and alibied, "I was off my game," his mother snapped: "You don't have a game! Get out and work harder and maybe, someday, you will."

Of course, he worked harder. He was always sensitive to the ethic around him. And he so much wanted her cooing praise. There was something special between the two of them, the way he'd make her giggle, even in church. Pres would turn and stare down the pew severely, but Dottie couldn't stop. Poppy was too much fun! And he adored her, admired her. He wrote, in 1985, in a Mother's Day tribute in *The Greenwich Times*:

"Physically she is a small woman, but she is made of mighty stuff. Nine months into her first pregnancy, she played baseball. Her last time up, she hit a home run, and without missing a base, continued right off the field to the hospital, to deliver Pres."

Yes, Pressie was the first—Prescott, Jr.—but he was different, a big boy, jovial and generous, not quite in the Walker mold. Pressie was a bruiser, a good football player, a lineman who loved to hit. But from birth, he had a problem with one eye that lent him, unjustly, the appearance of slowness. Then, playing football, he blew out a knee, and he was not so good at games anymore. It was her second boy, the one she named with her own father's names, George Herbert Walker, who had her gifts—the slender, supple form, the quickness, the charm. And she showed him in a thousand ways: he was The One. He was meant to win.

If she saved for him the bulk of that old Walker religion, he took it all, he grabbed for it. On Court One, again age twelve, with the family in attendance upon him, he played for the children's championship of the River Club. Early in the match, he turned to glower at the grandstand, and ordered his Aunt Mary, Uncle Herbie's wife, out of the stands. She was talking while he tried to play! That's how he got the nickname, in confirmation of the hope that had given him his name: *George Herbert Walker Bush*—Poppy—just like Pops.

By the time he played first base for Andover, no one else was in the running for captain. Poppy Bush was The One. Not that he was squawking for it: he was never loud, not the rah-rah sort. When you thought about it, he never seemed to mention himself. Maybe there were better ball players: better hitters probably, and Ed Machaj was a heck of a pitcher. But Ed came out of nowhere; everybody knew Poppy, he was a friend, always looking out for the other guy. One year, there was a Jewish kid named Ovie who left school when he didn't get tapped for the Greek societies. When they talked him into coming back, Poppy took him under his wing: brought him out for the ball team. One day a fly ball bounced off Ovie's head, into the left fielder's glove, and Poppy ran all the way out from first to congratulate Ovie on the assist.

But it was more than kindness, more than friends. Elly Vose, another starting pitcher, had almost as many friends; he was good-looking like Poppy, won as many class elections. But there was something about Bush: no one could really explain it. Part of it had to be the way he dealt with the coach, Follansbee, a strange little guy, and severe, sort of a stick: never spoke like a coach at all, but like a biology teacher, which he was. They said he'd been a pretty good catcher for Princeton in his day, but something happened to his legs: they were horribly twisted and bowed, with some kind of paralytic disease that never got talked about in those days. They called him Flop Follansbee behind his back, and some of the players never could get on with him. But Poppy was perfect, like he was with all the teachers. He wouldn't brownnose, or as they called it then, "suck," like some guys who had "drag" with the faculty. Poppy just fit in with them, like he belonged.

Still, there was something more, and this was about the way he played: it wasn't thought, or forethought—nothing studied. Just the reverse: it was release, almost the absence of self, in the focus on the game. He wanted *so hard* to be the best. They could see it before every game.

Infield practice was the last bit of business before a game, and old Flop Follansbee, he could run infield. Some coaches, who couldn't handle a bat, would just squib off grounders any-where, weak rollers, or high-bouncing, too-easy chops off the hard dirt in front of the plate. But Flop, with his professorial scowl and his poor twisted legs, was a fine hand with a bat and ball. He could hit with different hops and different speeds, make an infielder go to his left or right, just to the edge of his range: Flop could bring out the best in an infield. And he loved to get the best from Poppy Bush. Poppy had fine, soft hands, quick moves, and Flop loved trying to hit one by him. So the last bit of infield went like this: Flop would rap a grounder down to third, and the third baseman would throw home to the catcher. The catcher would fire back to third, where the third sacker went back to cover. Then the third baseman fired the ball home again, and ran for the bench. Then, onto the shortstop, who threw home . . . and the second baseman . . . if they had a sub, they'd always give him a chance, too. But finally, there was Poppy alone, crouched on the balls of his feet at first base. And all the fellows, whatever they were doing: fiddling with a mitt, tying spikes . . . everybody stopped, to watch this *thing* between Poppy and Flop. It was so . . . *intimate*; just between them, really. But it was also a touchstone for the game to come—a check of the hands that day. Flop would hit a grounder down to first, and Poppy would throw home. The catcher would throw back to first, and Poppy would fire back to the plate. But he wouldn't run to the bench. He'd charge the plate, right down the baseline, *streaking* in. And Flop would try to rap one by him. Never too hard, he made it fair. But you could see in the jawline of that crippled old coach: he was trying to beat the kid's beautiful hands. And what they remembered most was the way Poppy came at him—flying down the line with the air and the strain pulling his face taut— *laughing* with the pure joy of contest.

That's why he was The One for captain. It was the glint of Walker steel they saw. They wanted their team to be like that.

BY 1950, WHEN HE and Bar moved back to West Texas (over two years, Dresser Industries had moved him from Odessa, Texas, to a subsidiary in Huntington Park, California, and then to Bakersfield, then Whittier, then Ventura, then Compton, and, finally, back to Texas . . .), George Bush was not in the game—not really. He was only a salesman of drill bits.

The Scurry boom, a couple of counties away, to the northeast, was pumping out a fortune in oil, and the fortune was landing on Midland. Ideco, where Bush was employed, had its warehouse in Odessa. But Odessa was just a blue-collar town, home to roughnecks and equipment engineers (whose sons were perennial champs in the local high school football league). The West Texas offices of the major oil companies, and the brightest of the Yankee independents, were twenty miles northeast, in Midland. That was the place for Bush. . . . Problem was, finding a place. Midland now had *three* paved streets, but almost fifteen thousand souls packed into a town built for half that number. Oil was booming during the war, and for all the years thereafter. But it wasn't till a few years after the war that anyone, or anyone's money, could beg or buy enough wood, steel, or cement to build a block of office space, not to mention a thousand houses. So when the Bushes got back, there was no house. And now they were four. Little Georgie was almost ready for school, and back in one of those godforsaken California towns, he'd been joined by a baby sister, a beautiful little blonde whom George and Bar named Pauline Robinson Bush. Still, best they could do, for the moment, was a ratty motel called, by happenstance, George's Court.

Well, it was a wonderful adventure. They checked in, and every day, Barbara Bush would entertain two kids in one room, while George Bush drove the twenty miles southwest on Route 80—as bleak a drive as the U.S. offered; the sandstorms would take paint off your car—to his Ideco warehouse in Odessa, then back, at night, to his wife and kids in their motel. At last, someone built a tract of houses—wrong side of town, and no great shakes: all the same floor plan, 847 square feet (including carport), and an extra slab of cement, called a patio, that was buried in sand whenever the wind kicked up—but hell, they were houses. The tract got the nickname Easter Egg Row, for the way the developer painted these boxes—yellow, green, blue, or pink—mostly so you could tell which was yours. George and Bar bought one for $7,500—a bright blue egg, on a street called Maple. Of course, there wasn't a maple within five hundred miles.

But a lot of the independents were moving into Easter Egg Row. Red and Ferris Hamilton (brothers and proprietors of the Hamilton Oil Co.) lived one street over. Ashmun and Hilliard got an Easter Egg to share, couple of blocks away. John Overbey, who was a Texan, an independent, just starting out, got a house across Maple from George and Barbara Bush. And that was how Bush made his move. Even at the start, it was all about friends. George would get home around six at night, and sometimes,

Overbey would get back then, too. George would call him over for a drink, a cold martini on the patio (inside, if the dust was blowing), or maybe burgers from the backyard grill. He'd say to John, "Whad'ja do today?" And Overbey would tell his stories.

Overbey was a land man who'd scout out a likely property and try to cut a deal with the rancher who owned it, for a lease on the mineral rights. Overbey never had a pool of capital, so usually, he'd broker the lease, quick as he could, sell it to a major, or a big independent, who might be interested in drilling there. Sometimes John would take the money and run, maybe make a few hundred dollars over cost. Sometimes he'd sell the lease at cost, but carve out an override: that is, he'd keep a sixteenth or a thirty-second of any future production. The point was, he was in the game, and he always had a story to tell. . . . Maybe, that day, it was a tale of his travels to a dusty little town called Monahans, where he took the local abstractor out for a beer at the only joint in town, and found out Gulf Oil was buying, right there, on the edge of Rattlesnake Air Force Base. Or maybe he'd spent the day on his maps in his office, which was a single room in the old Scharbauer Hotel, which he shared with five fellows, one of whom, Charlie Roberts, always had a crap game going in the back. . . .

"Well, I had a hell of a day," Overbey would start out, after a few sips. "Took a trip downta Rankin . . . piece-a land looked pretty good. Looked like, on the map, like it might be open, so I went down to have a talk with this ol' rancher, Ad Neil . . ."

"Yeah?" Bush was soaking this stuff up.

"Yeah. So, I hunt him up, see if I could get a price outta

him. . . . Well, he's brandin' cattle . . . he wouldn't come outta damn corral. So I sat around on his fence half a day . . . *then* the sonofagun wants me buy him a beer, before he'll even *talk* to me."

"So did you?"

"Yep."

You could just about see Bush's eyes shining with the stories, the exotica of old Texas ranchers, the snooping around on the majors, the lure of the game. . . . Poor Bush only had a few stories about the guys he worked with at Ideco, and occasionally something funny some old roughneck would say at a well site, when George Bush stopped by to see if they'd need any bits. But that wasn't the game, no. . . . Overbey, even in his tiny way, was just where Bush wanted to be.

Pretty soon, with every story, he'd be asking Overbey a raft of questions. How much money could you make from a lease like that? Well, what could you have made, if you'd kept it, instead of brokering it? How much would it cost to drill one test there? . . .

Finally, one night, Bush said: "Geez, if I could raise some money, do you think we could do that? . . . Maybe get in business?" Overbey considered the proposition for about thirty seconds, before he said, yeah, he figured they could.

In the short run, money was equal or better than know-how. And money—to be precise, OPM, Other People's Money—was the calling card of the best young Yalie independents. Earle Craig was playing with Pittsburgh money. So were Ashmun and Hilliard. (H. T. "Toby" Hilliard was actually Harry Talbot Hilliard, of the Talbots of Fox Chapel, where the Mellons and friends had their houses.) Hugh and Bill Liedtke were keyed into oil money from Tulsa. Without outside money, you could spend a long while hustling leases before you could call any oil your own. So Overbey would be happy to show Bush everything he knew . . . Bush happily flew east to talk to Uncle Herbie. And Herbie Walker was *delighted* to place a bet on his favorite, Poppy, and to tell his Wall Street friends all about the doings of Pres Bush's boy. Pres himself went in for fifty thousand, along with Herbie, and some of Herbie's London clients, who all got bonds for their investment, along with shares in the new company— Bush-Overbey, they called it. Herbie Walker had decreed the name. After all, it was his money.

It was about $300,000, when they added it all together. So Bush and Overbey rented an office on the ground floor of the Petroleum Building—got it from Fred Turner, an independent who was moving up. But Bush-Overbey only took half—one room (the other was rented to insurance agents). A cautious player was George Bush. He wanted to be in the black every quarter. One room was enough, and a desk for each, two chairs, two typewriters, file cabinets, and a map rack. That was the sum total of equipment of the Bush-Overbey Oil Development Co. They weren't going to sit in the office, anyway.

Soon enough, Overbey had Bush out in his Chevy, plowing through the gritty wind out to Pyote, Snyder, and Sterling City. . . . Overbey had a few irons in the fire, and there was a piece of land right next to a dry hole that actually had a little show—just not enough to make a commercial well. But a half-mile south, now, maybe different story . . . you never could tell. No one was perfectly smart about this . . . it's like old H. L. Brown—Windy Brown, outta Fort Worth—used to say about the Scurry County boom, he used to say: "There was a time, if my land man even drove across that county, I'da fired him." See, you never could tell where the next boom was coming.

And Bush drank this all in, the lore, the lingo, all the names. He and Overbey scurried around, spending Herbie's money, trying to get it back as quick as they could. Kept a sixteenth here, a thirty-second there. . . . And now, Bush had maps under his arm as he breezed into The Spot for lunch. ("Just a bowla red, Helen. Gotta run. . . ." Bush was the first of the Yalies to go local with his diet—bowl of chili and crackers for lunch, chicken-fried steak at night.) Bush got to be a good hand with the records, and he was great on the personal side: people who came by the office to bullshit a minute, on their way somewhere, would find him, in the mornings, typing out friendly notes to people he met the day before. Sometimes, if you didn't have something he ought to hear, you couldn't pull him away from that typewriter for two minutes! He was always on the go, assiduous about the work. He was head of a family of four, steward to his father's money, and his uncle's, and his uncle's friends' . . . a man with rent to pay, a balance sheet to fret into the black . . . a man with a deal to promote—*Hey, this thing is surefire!* . . . a man with stories to tell ("Head geologist for the whole damn *region* gets up in the middle of the meeting . . . and pisses in the sink!") . . . a man twenty-seven years old . . . an independent oilman.

|4|

EVERYBODY SHOWED UP FOR touch football, except Hugh. It was the big event of the week. The fellows would gather Sunday afternoons, after church, at the high school practice field, mostly just to hack around, while the wives on the side-lines peered into one another's prams and talked about houses, schools, and kids. It was a family affair, start to finish. No one brought beer. And no one took the game seriously—save, per-haps, for Bush, who was always the quarterback, and called the plays, did the passing, and most of the running, too.

Sometimes, there was a real game—when they challenged the fellows from Lubbock, for instance. But even that was tongue-in-cheek. The Midland guys named the game the First Annual Martini Bowl. They named their team the Midland Mis-fits. They even printed a program, with ads from Bush-Overbey, and Liedtke & Liedtke, Attorneys at Law.

Not that Hugh was going to show up. Bill Liedtke would play football with the guys, or tennis, even golf, but brother

Hugh, the fellows used to say, only thought about deals: probably worked up deals in his sleep. Hugh and Bill Liedtke, as the ad said, operated as a law firm, but the only legal business they ever did was to bail a few of the Yalies out one night after they got liquored up in someone's apartment and went after the miller-moths with croquet mallets—busted up the walls pretty good. Anyway, three or four of the boys ended up at Sheriff Darnell's jail—and Big Ed's jail was not a place to spend a night, if you could help it. So Bill Liedtke came down to spring them. Of course, Hugh wasn't going to come . . . probably busy thinking up deals.

It wasn't that Hugh was unfriendly. Just seemed like when he was friendly, he always had something in mind. No, to be fair, it was the other way around: he always had something in mind; if he was friendly, that was just bonus. Anyway, you learned pretty quick that behind the deep drawl and jowly grin was a mind that was two or three sharp steps ahead of you, maybe a step or two ahead of what he was telling you. The Liedtke boys had grown up in the business—their father was a lawyer for Gulf, in Tulsa, and well connected there—and the way Hugh thought about the game was different from the rest of the Yalies. With the money from Tulsa, Hugh put Liedtke & Liedtke right into operation of wells. Hugh was buying and selling oil when most of the boys were hustling leases that *might* get drilled, and *might* have oil. Hugh Liedtke was building equity. He didn't talk about the Big One, the quick strike and a gusher of cash. He had a long-term, corporate view of the business. Hugh didn't mind buying into someone else's production. He'd try to work out a deal where he'd pay for the purchase, down the line, with proceeds from the oil he bought. Hell, if it came to that, Hugh wouldn't mind calling a broker in New York, to buy the stock of the company that owned a share of the partnership that owned the oil. He always saw five ways to skin the same cat. One of Hugh's stops in the Ivy League was the Harvard Business School, and what he brought to the West Texas oil fields was not romance, but a genius for finance.

The Liedtke brothers had an office across the street from Bush-Overbey, and, of course, George Bush made friends. Still, it came as a surprise in Midland when Bush let out word that he and Hugh—or, to be precise, the Liedtkes and Bush-Overbey— were going into business together. "I've been talking to Hugh," is the way Bush said it, "and we're going to go the corporate route." It seemed to the other fellows in Midland that with less than two years in the business, George Bush was a bit dewy for Hugh to pick as a partner. As usual, Liedtke had a different view. What he saw was a man who worked hard, who would work with him—maybe he wouldn't bring to the firm long experience, or deep knowledge of the business, but that would come. Hugh had the long haul in mind, and what Bush would bring, right away, was access to East Coast money. That was in the nature of Hugh's proposition: the Liedtkes would raise a half-million dollars, and Bush-Overbey would do the same. What they'd have was a real oil company—a million-dollar outfit—some staff, maybe a geologist . . . in the argot of the game, which Bush so enjoyed, "a little more muscle, a little more stroke."

That they did, when they joined up in March 1953, with

Hugh Liedtke as the new company president. George Bush would be vice president. . . .

"What should we call it? . . ."

President Hugh said it had to stand out in the phone book: "It oughta start with A . . . or a Z."

There was a movie playing that week in downtown Midland: *Viva Zapata!*, with Marlon Brando . . . so that's what they fixed on—Zapata, the name of a Mexican rebel *comandante*.

Hugh was right: it did stand out. And at twenty-eight, George Bush was not just in the game, he was on the map. In The Spot, or at the Ranch House, where the guys would kick back over dinner with a couple of drinks, people talked about Bush now in a different tone of voice. Zapata was a player—a clean million in equity. But Bush? . . . For the first time in his life, people talked about George Bush as a man whose résumé may have outpaced his attainments.

"Smartest thing he's done was to hook up with Hugh . . ." someone would say.

"Yep. Ol' Hugh, though: he's the one who makes the snowball . . . and he throws it."

"Yeah . . . bring s'more snow, George."

Even a year later, when the other independents learned, to their shock, to their admiration, and later still, to their envy, that Liedtke and Bush had bet it all on one roll of the dice—$850,000 on one lease—no one made much point of crediting Bush's steady faith, his assiduous work, his hyperactive friendliness . . . or even the good fortune that had followed him through three decades.

They leaned back in lawn chairs, around the barbecue in

someone's backyard, and shrugged: "Well," they said, "that's Hugh . . ."

Of course, by that time, no one who'd been close to Bush would have talked about his Great and Godly Good fortune— not that year . . . not at all.

THEY CALLED HER ROBIN, but her full name was Pauline Robinson Bush—named for Barbara's mother, who died in 1949, in a car accident, with her husband at the wheel. Marvin and Pauline Pierce had left home together one morning. Pauline took along a cup of coffee. As he drove, Barbara's father saw the coffee start to slide on the dash. He lunged to steady the cup, but he lost control of the car, hit a stone wall. He was hospitalized with broken ribs. Pauline was killed.

Bar did not go to New York for the funeral. She was seven months pregnant, and her father insisted she stay home and take care of herself. It was five days before Christmas when Bar gave birth to Robin. She would always remember the sight: it was the only birth for which Bar was awake, to watch, as her daughter came into the world.

Robin was still an infant when the Bushes moved back to Texas, just a toddler when George Bush swung full-time into business as an independent. Bar took care of the two kids, Georgie and Robin, in the house on Easter Egg Row, and then, in 1953, another child arrived, John Ellis Bush, whose name father George initialized: J.E.B. They called him Jebbie.

Among the Yalies in Midland, everybody kept having kids.

It seemed the natural way of things: at the time, Bar didn't think twice about her choices in life. It was decades later, when she looked back and labeled her state of mind in Midland as "dormant . . . just dormant." Or when, with a shrug, she dismissed all the might-have-beens and ought-to-have-beens with a smile of ironic self-mockery. "In a marriage," Bar said, "where one is so willing to take on responsibility, and the other so willing to keep the bathrooms clean . . . that's the way you get treated." (Of course, by that time, too, Bar had perfected her own power of mind-set: she could have gone back to college, she said. George would have applauded. But she did not go back, and did not look back. . . . "I think," Barbara Bush said, "people who regret something they did not do are liars.")

At the time, 1953, what she knew was, she was plenty busy, getting Georgie off to school in the morning, and getting Robin, who was still home all day, set up for play, and feeding the baby, Jebbie. . . . She'd wonder later, if she hadn't been so busy, would she have noticed sooner?

She never saw the little bruises on Robin's legs, or never observed them—every child got banged up playing. What she noticed, what worried her, was when Robin would not play. "What are you going to do today?" Bar asked her little girl.

"I'm either going to lie on the bed and look at books, or I'll lie on the grass, and watch the cars . . ."

That's when Bar took Robin to the pediatrician: Why should a three-year-old want to lie around all day? The doctor, a family friend, Dorothy Wyvell, didn't tell Bar her diagnosis. "Why don't you come back this afternoon, with George?" That rattled Barbara, sure enough.

She tracked down George at the Ector County Court-house, where he was digging into land records. That afternoon, Dr. Wyvell told them that Robin was very sick. She had leukemia.

It didn't sink in with George—not at first. He said: "Well, what do we do?" Dr. Wyvell started to cry.

"Well, what's the next *step?*" he insisted.

She told him there was no next step. Or, at least, she offered her advice, which was: do nothing. And tell no one. Just make Robin's time the best she could have. The child only had weeks to live.

George Bush, young man about business, could not believe it. He refused to believe it. He called his uncle, John Walker, a cancer specialist in New York, president of Memorial Hospital.

"I just had," Bush said, "the most ridiculous conversa-tion . . ." and he told Johnny Walker what Dr. Wyvell said.

"Why don't you bring her up here . . . have her looked at," Dr. Walker said. He'd arrange treatment by cancer specialists at the Sloan-Kettering Foundation. But, he warned his nephew, Dr. Wyvell might be right: leukemia was a killer. In '53, doctors had no sure way . . . in fact, little hope, of reversing it.

Bush kept replaying that conversation where he heard it was helpless, hopeless . . . he *could not do anything for his daughter.* . . . It was incredible. What was he supposed to do? Just take it? Sit on his hands?

"You'll never live with yourself if you don't treat her," John Walker told him over the phone. George, Bar, and Robin were on the plane for New York the next day.

That began a roller-coaster ride that went on for months. Bar was in New York, full-time, and George was father and mother in Texas, until the weekends, when the boys would stay with neighbors while George flew to New York to join his wife and daughter. The doctors at Sloan-Kettering gave Robin an experimental drug—it was new that year . . . no one could promise . . . but she got better . . . she could eat, she sat up, she could play . . . doctors called it remission. And after a couple of months, Bar and Robin were home in Midland. . . . But then the child started to sink again, and the drug was no help, the roller-coaster screamed downhill, Robin and Bar went back to New York, and George was flying back and forth.

It was hell for all of them, but George was the one who just could not stand it. Bar made a rule that there would be no crying in front of Robin: Bar meant to make her daughter's days happy ones. And she did: Bar stayed with Robin hour after hour, playing with her, reading to her, tickling her, talking, holding her as she slept, smoothing her blond hair. Barbara Bush stayed with her daughter through it all. Like an oak in the wind, she was tossed, but she would not be moved. No one in Midland, or in New York at the hospital, ever saw Barbara Bush cry, through seven months, while her daughter slipped away. George could not sit and take it like that. He marveled at his wife's strength—it was beyond strength, it was heroic, an act of will and love that he could not match. He could not look at his daughter without fighting tears, and a helpless rage, or despond that he could not bear. He was so grateful to have work to do, places to be, people to see. He'd burst out of that house in the morning like a man trapped in smoke lunges toward fresh air. Sometimes, he'd stop at church to say a prayer. Then he'd immerse himself in the game, the cares of the living.

Of course, he could not follow Dr. Wyvell's counsel of silence, either: everyone in Midland knew . . . all their friends, and their families. Some of the friends in Midland gave blood for Robin's transfusions. When Bar and Robin were home from New York, Betty Liedtke, Hugh's wife, would come to the house almost every day. And she'd cook, hoping to tempt Robin to eat . . . and tempting Barbara, who might not have thought of food for herself. In New York, Barbara had her own family to support her. She stayed with George's grandparents, just blocks from the hospital. Her old friends, and George's, were everywhere around. From Greenwich, George's mother, Dorothy Bush, sent a nurse to Texas, to be with George and the boys. And Prescott Bush, newly elected to the United States Senate, called Bar one day, to come out with him in Connecticut. He said he wanted her help, picking out his gravesite. And gently, he led her through the cemetery, until they found a lovely spot . . . a place, Prescott said, where he would be comfortable . . . and there he planted a hedge, *a bush* . . . of course, that was just his tender way of making a place for Robin.

Uncle Johnny Walker was at the hospital every day. He was more than counsel, he was inspiration: his own career as a surgeon had been cut short, a few years before, by polio, and doctors said he'd never walk again, but John Walker not only made a second career in business at the G. H. Walker firm, he also served medicine as president of Memorial Hospital—and with crutches he got around New York, every day, on the subway. In the end, in October, it was Dr. John Walker who tried to tell Bar: she could let Robin go. The girl was failing, the cancer drugs had eaten holes in her stomach. She was bleeding inside. She was very weak. The Sloan-Kettering doctors wanted to operate: they thought they might stop the bleeding . . . anyway, they knew so little about these cases, they wanted to try. . . . Bar was twenty-eight years old, and this, she had to decide alone. George was in the air, on his way to New York.

"You don't have to do it," Dr. Walker told Bar.

But Bar felt she had to. Those doctors were half killing themselves, trying to save Robin. And there was always hope—wasn't there? She gave the go-ahead, and the surgeons went to work.

But Robin never came out of the operation. George was there that night, when Robin died. She was two months short of her fourth birthday. George and Bar did not bury her, but left her for the doctors at Sloan-Kettering. They wanted her death to mean something for other children who would face this, in years to come.

After Robin died, the world changed for Barbara Bush. All at once, the unfairness, the pain and loss, came crashing down on her and she was without strength, without will. It was George now who took her in hand. And he did what he thought best: the day after Robin died, it was George who went to the hospital, to thank everybody who had worked on his child. And then, in Rye, he took Bar to the club, and they played golf.

Barbara was lost in her grief. It was only George who kept her going. After Robin's death, he was released, to act, to keep moving. He knew so well how to do that. And he would not let his wife sink into her mourning. They had to go on, he told her. But for a while, she did not know how. He was like a man holding on to her at the cliff edge: they had to keep moving, to live—there were the boys . . . there was him! There was their life, still, to live! . . . In later years, she always gave him credit for saving her, for saving them. Somewhere, she learned a statistic: two-thirds of the couples who lose a child, as they did, end up divorced from the strain and the grief, the guilt and blame . . . but not George and Barbara Bush. They were stronger, and she always blessed him for that. Sometimes, when she thought back, she would tell of the critical moment for her . . . it was so strange, and small, when she told it, she was sure no one would quite understand, but that was the instant she turned away from the cliff edge.

It was the day of the memorial service, and the house was filling with friends and family, and Bar was upstairs getting ready, in the bedroom . . . but she wasn't getting ready. She could not. She could not *get* herself to go down those stairs, to face all those people, and have the sad wound in her opened to them . . . she just *could not* go down there. Did he know? Hard to say. He was not urging her, or even looking at her. George was standing at the window, looking over the yard and the walk, his lanky form silhouetted in the light . . . as he watched Bar's sister, Martha, and her husband, Walter Rafferty, coming toward the front door. And he said, as if to himself, just one of his wry play-by-plays . . . with a hint of an Irish brogue: "Ah, here come the O'Raffertys. It's goin' to be a helluva wake!"

With that, somehow, it came to her, penetrated her pain: there he was, her George, and he was so . . . all right. They both were. They had so much. . . . It didn't stop the pain. Back in

Texas, the pain would be a physical presence, an ache inside . . . but she would go on.

As for George, he seemed never to doubt, never to waver, from the instant Robin was lost to them. He always seemed to have the articles of faith he'd taken from his mother's breakfast readings. Life was good. Life was for the living. Good things happened to good people. It wasn't so much what he said, as how he lived. The point was, to keep moving, doing, turned ever outward: when Bar and he flew back to Midland, George Bush did not take them home, but directly from the airport to the houses of their friends—all over town, visiting friends. . . . He said it would be hard for people to come to them, in that situation, and he wanted so much to tell people, thank you.

AND HE WAS MOVING. That was the moment he and Hugh Liedtke rolled the dice. There was a big swatch of land in Coke County, about eighty miles from Midland, and Sun Oil had wells, producers, on a parcel just to the east. Zapata bet $850,000—for all practical purposes, Hugh and George bet everything—on the proposition that a huge pool of oil extended west under eight thousand acres of sand.

Two-thirds of that lease, called the Jameson field, was owned by a Wichita Falls outfit called Perkins-Prothro. But the other third was held by an oilman named Green, who worked out of San Angelo. When Green wanted to sell his interest, Hugh Liedtke wanted that lease. Problem was, a couple of independents out of Midland beat him to it. Bob Wood and Leland

Thompson got in there and made a deal with Green a week ahead of Zapata. But Hugh always saw five ways to skin the same cat: he and George Bush worked out a deal to pay Wood and Thompson $50,000 and *then* carry them for a quarter interest. . . . Zapata had its deal.

How could they be so sure? They could not. You never really knew until you drilled each hole. They had some geologists working for them now, and there was a senior geologist, just retired from Gulf, whom George and Hugh kept taking to lunch . . . but still, you could never *know*. Call it instinct, or faith (good things happen . . .), but no one among the independents in Midland ever bet it all like that. No one in their crowd had done that before.

So they drilled—Perkins-Prothro was the official operator on-site—and probably sank another hundred or a hundred twenty-five thousand on that . . . and they hit.

So they drilled again . . . and they hit. And drilled again . . . and they hit. The way books were kept in the game, there were two classes of drilling expense. The first was capital expense, which was the wellhead, and the pump, the pipe and like tangibles, all of which could be depreciated over a ten-year term. The second class was called intangibles, and covered things like rental of a drilling rig, special mud to lubricate the drill bits, diesel fuel to operate the rig, labor costs . . . and all of that was written right off the top of your taxes. With a setup like that, it almost paid you to keep drilling.

So they did . . . another hole . . . and they hit. And another, and another . . . and they hit.

In the span of a year, Zapata and Perkins-Prothro drilled

seventy-one holes . . . and seventy-one of them hit. By the end of
that year, they were pumping out 1,250 barrels of oil each day, at
that time worth about $1.3 million a year. By the time the Jame-
son field was fully drilled, the partnership had bored 127 holes
. . . and 127 wells produced.

George and Hugh were the first of the Midland independents to be worth a million apiece. All the fellows talked about
them . . . well, mostly they talked about Hugh. It was hard to
talk *to* him anymore. Never around—too busy. George Bush
they still saw—hadn't changed a bit. Except now, you wouldn't
find him hanging around The Spot. He might take his lunch at
the Petroleum Club. Sometimes he'd go with John Overbey—
probably neither one was a member, but they'd go on Bush's
invite. Overbey had dropped out of Zapata—didn't have much
taste for the corporate business, went back to what he knew,
which was land work, and leasing . . . dropped off too early, as
it happened. He lost out. But George Bush never lost a friend.
Bush also teamed up with Bob Wood, one of the fellows who
snuck in a week ahead on that Jameson deal, and those two
started the Commercial Bank and Trust Company. Bush wasn't
quite thirty years old. Meanwhile, Zapata built its own office
building in Midland. And hired more staff . . . a little more
stroke. And George and Bar got a new house, and then another,
a bigger house. And then, they were the first of their crowd to
have a swimming pool. . . . And George Bush really liked that—
everybody came over.

5

GEORGE BUSH WAS STILL in Midland, in the big house on Sentinel, the last of George and Bar's homes in West Texas, when he first mentioned to a friend what he meant to do with his life.

It was George and C. Fred Chambers in the kitchen . . . the kids and wives were at the pool . . . no one else in the house that day. Bush said: "You ever had any sake?"

"No, let's try it," Chambers said. "Looks like a warm beer can to me."

"Well, that's how you drink it, I guess."

So they popped open this rice wine, and started feeling warm, pretty good . . . sitting at the kitchen table, talking oil, like they always did—Bush and Chambers were in deals together— when Bush said: "Fred, what do you wanna do? . . . I mean, for the rest of your life."

"Well, I'm here . . ." Fred said. "Oil bidness, I guess . . ."

Tell the truth, it caught him off guard. He never expected the question, not from Bush. He always figured George was like

him—like everybody—just meant to hit the biggest field *ever* . . .
pile it up . . . find the next one.

"You know what I think," Bush said. That wasn't a question.
"I think I want to be in politics, serving, you know, public office."

Fred took that in, nodded: "Well, I think that's great," he
said. "I thought of being a teacher or something, where you do
something for people . . ."

But Fred could tell, as he said it, that Bush wasn't just thinking about it. Bush had thought. Fred didn't ask him how, or
when . . . it just seemed settled. Bush'd do it, somehow. Fred
didn't have to ask him why. He knew why. George had always
felt that way about his dad.

PRESCOTT BUSH HAD THE old-fashioned idea that a man who'd
been blessed had a duty to serve. He'd always had public office
somewhere in his mind. But what Pres saw was the service, the
office. He did not take easily or quickly to the politics required to
get there.

He first considered a run for Congress in '46, while Poppy
was at Yale . . . but his partners at Brown Brothers Harriman
took a dim view of the crowded House chamber. "Well, Pres,"
one of the Harrimans said, "if it were the Senate, we'd surely
back you . . . but the House? We need you here more than the
House needs you." And that was the end of that notion: there
were no disputes among partners in the Brown Brothers' paneled
boardroom.

So it wasn't till 1950 that he filed for office, and then for the Senate, and he ran nose to nose with a Democrat incumbent. But the Sunday before the vote, Drew Pearson predicted on his network radio show that Prescott Bush would lose the Connecticut Senate race . . . *because it had just been revealed that Bush was president of the Birth Control League.* Well, it didn't happen to be true, but more than half the voters in Connecticut were Catholics (state law actually prohibited the use of contraceptives), and Pres was denounced at every mass—it must have cost him ten thousand votes . . . anyway, just enough votes: he lost by eleven hundred, and his dream of service in the nation's best club was dashed. Two years later, he filed for the Senate again, but this time he narrowly lost the nomination to an upstate businessman named Bill Purtell, and Pres had to give up his dream: he'd run twice, he'd lost. He was finished.

But then—a Great and Godly Good stroke of fortune, or rather several, a Blessed Confluence: that same June, 1952, the senior Senator, Brien McMahon, died in office. Pres was handed the nomination . . . he had to campaign only two months in a special election . . . and, in the Eisenhower landslide, he beat young Congressman Abe Ribicoff by almost thirty thousand votes. At last, he would take up residence and the duties of a statesman in Washington. Moreover, as he'd won a special election, to replace a Senator deceased, he could take up his duties the day after the vote: he did not have to wait for the new Congress (unlike Purtell, who had knocked Pres out of the *regular* election), and became, instantly, the *senior Senator* from Connecticut, a man of standing in the Capitol.

In fact, by Blessed Confluence, Prescott Bush found life in the capital almost unimaginably congenial. There was the fact that he'd backed the Eisenhower wing in the late Republican political wars, and so found friends in the White House—like Sherman Adams, the President's right-hand man. Then, too, Pres was one of the few golfers among GOP Senators—surely, the best golfer—and so he was often Ike's playing partner: that was most congenial. And then, too, Pres had been friends forever with Bob Taft—met him years ago, as sons of good family will, in Cincinnati (served on Yale's board with him, since '44)—and as the GOP had taken back the Senate in Ike's landslide, well, Pres's friend Bob Taft was the Leader of the Senate. And it did not hurt that Taft's son Bill was a professor at Yale in those years, and so a constituent of Pres Bush, and when Bill Taft decided he'd like to be Ambassador to Ireland, it was Pres Bush who called his friend Sherm Adams, and pushed the nomination through the White House. And surely that was easier because Foster Dulles, at State, was a friend (lawyer to Brown Brothers Harriman, for quite a while) . . . as were the men at Treasury, and Commerce, of course—men of business whom Pres had known for years, and very congenial fellows all. And when there was friction between the Republican Senate and the Eisenhower administration (a good deal of friction—Ike was not really a pol, and notwithstanding his golf, not really a clubable man), it was Pres who hosted a dinner at the Burning Tree Country Club, to get all the fellows together—brought a wonderful quartet down from Yale to sing (Ike never forgot that, nor that Pres's son Johnny sang bass)—and things went along much better after that.

In all, it was a splendid time for a gentleman of business and grand personal qualities to serve in the Senate. And though he did not leave a long list of laws that bore his name, Pres was welcomed in the capital's councils of power, to have a look (perhaps a quiet word, here and there) on the most important and interesting matters in the Eisenhower years. He was such a sure-footed man, so impressive, so steady in his personal code . . . that people listened to Pres, though he was new in the Senate. He was a good ally—his word was his bond—and a good friend: they all noticed that. When Sherman Adams ran into such trouble with that Goldfine, and the vicuna coat . . . well, for a while, Pres and Dottie were the only ones who'd still have Adams to dinner. Pres took a leading role in the censure of Senator Joseph McCarthy— alas, that fellow did step over the line . . . but when McCarthy fell sick, in 1955, Pres was the last (maybe the only) member of the Senate to stop by the hospital and wish Joe well.

In general, Pres took to the job with grace, and assiduity. He traveled the world for a blue-ribbon commission for international trade. Later, as a member of the Armed Services Committee, he'd descend in a small plane onto the deck of some U.S. carrier, where he'd spend a few days with the officers, at sea. That was always most interesting. Meanwhile, each week, from the Senate studio, he'd make a TV broadcast for distribution in his state. (As a banker, in the thirties, Pres had helped launch CBS, and his friends there, Bill Paley and Frank Stanton, counseled him to do all the TV he could.) At the same time, he was a stickler for responding, personally, to every letter or telegram. Most weeks, he'd sign a thousand letters. He acknowledged every invitation, every contribution. His office worked six days a week, and Pres did, too. He spoke at a hundred public schools in the state, kept in touch with town officials, state officials, labor unions, the insurance companies of Hartford, the manufacturers of Bridgeport . . . he meant to show that they were his interest, that he was, as he put it, "a lift-up and bear-down sort of Senator." And though he had a bitter reelection campaign against the well-known Thomas Dodd, Pres made splendid use of TV—he was quite good with that camera now—and won by the largest plurality ever attained in Connecticut.

After that . . . and after 1960, when things did not quite work out for Dick Nixon . . . well, Pres wondered, as every Senator must, how he'd do, how he'd feel, at the other end of Pennsylvania Avenue. Yes, the thought occurred . . . he'd been around the White House quite a bit, what with the pleasant friendship he'd had with Ike. It did not seem oversized, or strange . . . and there was no clear standard-bearer for the party, not from the mainstream, anyway. Yes, the thought occurred . . .

But things did not work out that way. Pres's own health was shaky, his doctors were quite firm about slowing him down. He would be sixty-seven when he'd have to run for reelection. And even Dottie, he knew—though she'd never say a word—was dreading the effort to come. Well, he had to take stock, and he did. He came to a firm decision: he would retire. He just could not drag Dottie through another campaign. Maybe if his health were better . . . maybe, if Kennedy hadn't beat Nixon by a hundred thousand votes in Connecticut . . . maybe, if Abe Ribicoff meant to stay, content, in the Governor's chair . . . maybe, if Pres had begun his own service as a younger man—well, surely . . . but no.

And so, with regret (with a stoic sorrow that would only grow, as his health improved), Senator Bush announced he was stepping down. He removed his name from consideration. That was the end of politics for him—an end, he was convinced, that came too soon. And that was 1962.

IT WAS THAT SPRING, '62, when Houston's party leaders came to Bush's house for lunch. Oh, they were in an awful bind.

The GOP was growing in Houston—in fact, it was on the rise all over Texas. (They'd even elected a Senator in '61, when LBJ had to give up his seat to assume the Vice Presidency. They got that runty professor, John Tower—a couple of party leaders held him down on a table and shaved off his little Hitler mustache—and sent him out as a single-shot Republican against a field of about seventy Democrats . . . and he won!)

But the problem was *how* the Republican Party was growing. The GOP had papered the state with its new slogan, "Conservatives Unite!" Of course, no one dreamed what that might mean. They *had* pried the right wing loose from the Democrats. The party meetings were bigger than ever, but those new Republican voters—they were extreme, on the fringe, they were . . . well, they were *Birchers*!

These . . . these *nuts*! They were coming out of the woodwork! (Actually, they came out of a couple of fringy churches in the working-class suburb of Pasadena.) These people talked about blowing up the United Nations, about armed revolt against the income tax. They had their guns loaded at home, in case commies should appear that night. . . . Well, you can imagine how upsetting it was to *decent* Republicans—that is, to the lime-green pants crowd, who'd organized the GOP in Texas about the same time they'd founded their country clubs.

In fact, in the last Party convention, in Houston, right there in Harris County, it was everything decent folk could do just to hold on to the leadership. Jimmy Bertron was their candidate for county chairman—such a fine young man!—the man who'd shaved John Tower and steered him to the Senate. But the Birchers poured in; they were packing the place! (Bob Crouch, one of the old-line faithful, had to head over to the black side of town "to round up some Toms" . . . at least they'd vote right.)

Well, it was a bitter fight to the end. But when all the ballots were counted, Bertron held on—by sixteen votes! . . . Landslide Bertron!

The Party was saved!

But not for long. Now, in '62, Jimmy Bertron wanted to move to Florida. In fact, he was leaving, and leaving the chair . . . the Party was up for grabs again.

That's why they came to George Bush.

"George, you've got to help us! You've got to run for chairman!"

Well, wasn't it great, how it worked out?

ACTUALLY, BUSH HAD HIS hands full—business, and all. Not that he was making a prophet of Fred Chambers, trying to pile it up . . . no, he was not that way. That was more his old partner's style—Hugh Liedtke—now, there was a man who gave new meaning to the verb "amass."

That's really why they'd split up—Hugh and George divvied up Zapata in 1958. See, Hugh was all for acquisition, corporate takeovers, buying production. He liked business. But George, he was more for the hunt, the future, the cutting edge, exploration. He liked the *oil game.* In effect, they split the company in half, and Hugh kept Zapata's land operations, and George took over Zapata Off-Shore, which was a subsidiary they'd created to drill for oil under the ocean bed. That was the future, according to Bush.

(Of course, he was dead wrong. Oh, offshore went fine— grew into a giant industry—that part was true. But the future, turned out, lay with the corporate takeover boys, and with Liedtke, who soon acquired South Penn Oil, and turned that into Pennzoil, and—well, it was just a pity that Uncle Herbie and his money men went with Poppy on that split.)

Anyway, it was the offshore business that carried Bush to Houston—and it wasn't any life of leisure. By 1962, Bush had four rigs to drill on the seabed; each cost several million dollars, and each had to keep working. He had more than two hundred people on his payroll, maybe ten times as many shareholders to consider. He had farm-outs of ocean-floor leases from the majors, he had contracts to drill, schedules to keep; he had business possibilities everywhere in the world there was oil under water. He had insurance, he had accountants, he had lawyers, bankers—he had debt. He had storms at sea that threatened his equipment . . . he had five kids who had to get educations . . . he had an ulcer.

So he looked at those Houston Republicans who came to lunch, at those desperate souls who wanted him for county chairman, and he said: "Well, jeez, sure! I mean, if you want . . ."

WELL, AFTER THAT, THE pace of the Party picked up—everyone could feel it. The big difference was, the chairman *worked:* out every night, somewhere in the county, trying to find Republican election judges, or trying to find black precinct captains. No Republican chairman had ever been *seen* in the black precincts. They were thirty-to-one for the Democrats. But Bush wouldn't give up. He'd stand on some broken-down front porch, talking up the *two-party system*, how that was *good* and *right for the country* . . . until people inside either signed up or told him to get lost. Come Election Day, a lot of those captains would just take the money, stick it in their pockets . . . but George had them on the lists that he updated each week.

Most nights, he'd stop at headquarters, and the place seemed to swell with enthusiasm. Sometimes, Barbara would come, too—she'd stuff envelopes with the lady volunteers—but more often, it was only George. Aleene Smith, party secretary, would have everything ready on his desk. George would read and sign the letters, sign the checks, write his memos, and clear the desk before he went home.

HQ was a dump on Audley Street, but Bush soon moved it to better quarters, a nice old house on Waugh Drive, near Allen Parkway. (Of course, people said he picked the place because it was on his way home from his office atop the Houston Club—but that's just how people are.) The house was perfect—volunteers had tables in the living room, the committee could meet on the side porch, or in the dining room. George put his office upstairs, in the front bedroom, and he fixed it up fine. He got the money from the first Neighbor to Neighbor Fund Drive—the kind of thing he used to do for the Midland Red Cross, a civic exercise. He got some local business friends to donate computer time, and he made lists of all the Republicans in the county. Then the precinct chairmen got the lists, just like they would for an election—but this time, for quarters and dollar bills. They raised more than ninety thousand dollars, probably double what the party ever had. Then he used some of that money to support the campaign of Bill Elliot, who became the first city councilman ever elected by the GOP—and that put more fire into the troops.

The troops were mostly women in those days, battle-hardened matrons who'd kept the flame when the whole county convention wouldn't fill a good-sized coffee shop, who'd fought like cheetahs for the last few years to keep the Bircher goofballs out of the office. Of course, the ladies loved George, adored him. He was so young, for one thing—just thirty-eight—and eager, enthusiastic . . . and so handsome, the way he'd stand up, tall and slender in front of the room, and talk about what the Republican Party *meant*, with his high voice coming from up behind his nose, with that foreign eastern accent. Well, it was like Cary

Grant, or David Niven, come to work at the office. And that was just the start: then they found out how kind he was, how interested in them, grateful for their work, eager to include them, to be their friend . . . he was so *decent*!

Too decent for politics.

They all agreed about that.

They had to protect him.

Poor George didn't even know who was a nut, and who was out to get him. He was so nice to those Birchers . . . really, sometimes, you wanted to shake him by the neck!

He couldn't see, the nuts *hated him*. They could *smell* Yale on him. Of course, it didn't help, the first time Jimmy Bertron introduced him to the executive committee: "Good friend of mine," Jimmy said. "George Bush . . . only thing wrong with him, he beats me at tennis."

Yuk. Yuk.

You could have heard a pin drop. Gene Crossman, one of the good ol' slimeball right-wingers, said: "Thass it, dammit. I'm not votin' for 'nother country-club asshole. Y'kin jus' fergit it."

But George had the idea they should all get along. He thought he could talk to the Birchers, make them *like* him . . . once they got to know him. They were probably good folks, underneath. He was always saying stuff like "We all have the same *basic* goals . . ." He couldn't seem to get what was basic to the Birchers: being rid of *him* and everyone like him . . . like *Eisenhower, Rockefeller* . . . like all those rich, pointy-head, one-worlder, fellow-traveler, eastern-Harvard-Yale-country-club-Council-on-Foreign-Relations *commie dupes*!

No, George tried to talk to them, reason with them, involve them. He *wanted* them to come, participate, join the committees. He wanted to know them, to see their lives, to let them see his. He had them over to his house, for meetings, for breakfasts with him and Bar. He had *everybody* over to his house on Briar Drive. He wanted to share, see, him and Bar—they made everybody feel so *comfortable* there. It was a fine, big house in the Tanglewood section, but nothing austere about it: everything was comfy, the sofas, the chairs. You'd come in, sit down, and George would serve drinks, padding around with no shoes, in a sport shirt. The dog would come around—that dog who'd get crippled, psychosomatically paralyzed, any time George and Bar went away. That was always a joke with the Bushes. And the kids would be running around, in and out of doors that led from the family room to the backyard. They were all still in school— Doro was only three or four years old—but they were good kids, who'd always say hello to grown-ups. On the wall, there was the portrait of Robin, the little girl who died. You felt a part of it all, even when you just came for a meeting. Of course, that's how George wanted you to feel.

Wanted *everyone* to feel: sure, some of those folks had extreme ideas. But Bush was not one to judge a man on account of his *ideas* . . . no. So, first thing, he put out a half-page memo, telling *everybody:* no more name-calling. "We're all Republicans, and we're not going to divide ourselves, calling anyone 'crazies,' or 'nuts' . . ." He didn't want to *hear* the word "nut." (So what they did, they started calling everybody "Kernel" . . . Kernel Smith, or Kernel Crouch, or Kernel Nancy Palm, better known as Kernel Napalm . . . it was Bob Crouch who started it—had to have *some* word for "nut.")

Then—this was '63—Bush decided the Birchers had to have jobs, they had to be *involved*, he was going to give them *precincts!*

"George, you don't know these people," Sarah Gee, one of the stalwart ladies, tried to tell him. "They mean to kill you!"

"Aw, Sarah," he'd say. "There's some good in everybody. You just gotta find it."

The first was a gal named Randy Brown. George made them vote to give her a precinct. Sarah was livid. All the ladies were furious. Randy didn't even hide her contempt! What got into Bush? Couldn't he see? . . . He made them vote her in, and they were coming out of the dining room, after the vote, and he was coming downstairs from his office, at that moment. There he was, beaming like a kid, as he said, "Congratulations!" . . . Randy stared up at him, not a hint of a smile, and said: "George, you'll rue the day you made 'em put me on."

No, HE COULDN'T SEE. Or didn't choose to. For one thing, he was too excited. There were too many good things happening. Good things for the party. Good things for him. All those new friends! Nice things people said . . . they were talking to him about the U.S. Senate!

Sure, it'd be tough, but he had a shot . . . if he could unite the party, draw some conservative Democrats . . . he'd unite them all around his person. They had to like *him* . . . he knew they would. Goldwater would unite the party—just the kind of Republican the Texas GOP could get behind. Hell, just the man for Bush to get behind! He was so un-eastern, un-monied, un-moderate. Bush was big for Goldwater in '64—whole hog for Barry!—no one was going to out-conservative George Bush.

Tell the truth, Bush's program wasn't in conflict with Goldwater's . . . as Bush didn't have a program. Sure, he was conservative—a businessman who had to meet a payroll—but that's about as far as it went, on policy. One of the first times he ever made a speech—some little town just south of Houston— one good ol' boy stood up in the crowd and asked Bush for his position on the Liberty Amendments. Well, Bush didn't have a clue about the Liberty Amendments. (They were a series of Bircher constitutional changes to get America out of the UN, repeal the income tax, abolish the Federal Reserve, a few other things like that.) Poor Bush was helpless. He turned to Barbara, the eastern matron, busy at her needlepoint onstage . . . no help there. So Bush said he hadn't had time, yet, to *study* those important amendments . . . but he certainly would.

Tell the truth, Bush wasn't much for programs, one way or the other. It wasn't that he wanted to do anything . . . except a good job. He wanted to *be* a Senator. . . . Just about the time he was thinking it over, about to announce his big move, there were stories in the paper—front page, it was awful!—about this little girl in the Houston public housing, sleeping on the floor, who'd got bitten by a rat! God, what a shame! . . . Bush didn't think about a program for housing, or maybe calling that councilman he helped to elect—propose a rat eradication plan! No, he called home, that afternoon:

"Bar? . . . You think we could give that family our baby bed?"

And they did. That very evening, George came home, packed up that bed, and took it right over.

That's why Bush was gonna win the election: concern for the common man. Common values . . . common decency. That's what people had to know about him . . . that, and the fact—Bush could *see* it, everywhere—the Democrats were out of touch. They'd held on to Texas since the Civil War! They'd lost sight of the common folk . . . that was Bush's secret weapon. The Democrats were split, right down the middle. The incumbent Senator was an old-fashioned liberal, Ralph Yarborough—out of step with the new Texas, George Bush's Texas. The state was changing—Bush knew it, just as surely as Nixon beat Kennedy in Houston, last time—but old Yarborough hadn't got the wake-up call. He was still traveling the state in his white suit and big white hat, promising the world. . . . Bush *knew* he could take him. Jeez, even Lyndon couldn't stand Yarborough (Yarborough called Johnson "power mad"). And now that LBJ was Vice President—that had to hurt Yarborough, didn't it? Johnson would be running with Kennedy again—that was the good news for the Democrats. But people didn't vote straight ticket anymore . . . LBJ on the ballot might even *help* Bush . . . *everybody* knew how Lyndon hated Yarborough.

So Bush started talking it up—Senator!—just to friends, at the start. And there were more than a couple who suggested that maybe he ought to go easy, take it slow . . . maybe run for office once, you know, something local, or *Congress* . . . how 'bout Congress first? But Bush didn't want to hear that. He was going to announce, September '63. He'd do it with a splash! He knew where he belonged—in the U.S. Senate. Jeez, almost a year now, and his father *still* regretted leaving the Senate.

Oh, God—Dad! . . . Big Pres could be a problem!

Prescott Bush was not a Goldwater man. In fact, he was just the kind of fellow that the eastern wing was counting on to get behind *someone decent* . . . like Rockefeller, or Lodge—or Bill Scranton . . . someone to stop that *nut*, Goldwater. In fact, just a year or so after retirement, Pres would have liked nothing better than to keep his hand in, at least in Connecticut.

But George called, asked him flat-out: Don't do it! It was bad enough, they were talking in the churches of Pasadena about Bush's father, the Senator, a *member* of the Council on Foreign Relations! If he came out against Goldwater . . .

And so, Pres had to swallow it down, for his son. The torch had passed . . . to young George. It was his turn. Prescott Bush sat on his hands in '64. The whole campaign through, he could barely say a word. He confirmed and completed his sad political exile.

And in Texas, George Bush started campaigning in earnest. He'd have to have men in the field—area chairmen! It was time to make his move—so he called a meeting . . . and, as his first appointment, he turned to that slimeball Bircher, Gene Crossman, and appointed *him* to head up East Texas.

Well, that was too much for the ladies. One of the veterans,

Linda Dyson, heard about Crossman, and she marched up the stairs of HQ, right to the front bedroom, George's office . . . where she flung open the door, and shouted in Bush's frozen face:

"George Bush! Y'know what your problem is? . . . You don't know the difference between a common man and a *common* common man."

BUT HE KNEW HOW to make a man feel special—and that's what he did, all over the state. Bush had a four-man primary, and one of his opponents was Jack Cox, another young comer, a hot stump speaker who'd already run for Governor (and gave John Connally a run for his money).

Bush—well, he wasn't much on the stump. He'd get cranked up, dive into a twisty river of a sentence, no noun, a couple or three verbs in a row, and you wouldn't know where he was headed—sometimes for minutes at a stretch, while his hands sawed and pulled at the air, smacked on the podium, drew imaginary lines and boxes without name, without apparent reference to what he was talking about, which you couldn't exactly tie down, unless you caught a key word, now and then, like "Sukarno," or "taxes," or "lib-rull" (that one came up a lot), although you could tell it really hacked him off, the way his voice rose through the octaves—until he emerged on the other side of the Gulf of Mexico, red in the face, pleased as hell with himself, spluttering out the predicate, or maybe the direct object of that

second-last verb, and a couple more random words that had occurred to him in the meantime, and you could see he cared, and
it all went together in his mind, but it wasn't clear exactly how,
or what it was he thought was so damned *important.*

Fortunately, there weren't many speeches required in the
primary, which was a meet-the-folks affair in most Texas towns,
where you could still get the registered Republicans into a single
room. He did covered-dish dinners, cocktail parties, barbecues
. . . and he was beautiful. He'd talk to everybody one-on-one,
and they loved him. He was so eager to know about them! And
he already had party-official friends, after his year as chairman;
and he knew all the oilmen, and a lot of fellows in business; and
old neighbors, guys who'd drifted down from Yale . . . no one
ever slipped off his screen. And after every dinner, every barbecue or picnic, Bush'd get back on his plane and ask his area
chairman: "Who're the ten people I wanna thank in Pecos?"
And he'd do those ten notes before he was halfway home. Back
in Houston, he'd do a few dozen more, banging them out on his
own machine, with typos and x-outs and other endearing steno
foibles, all explained in the top-right corner of the note, where
he'd put: "Self-typed by GB."

Well, it worked like a charm. As did the Bush Bandwagon,
a busful of friends dropped off in some neighborhood, working
door-to-door from lists the volunteers had prepared . . . and not
just in River Oaks or Tanglewood, but anywhere there were Republicans. They'd work in couples—safer that way—and Bar'd
go with George's friend, a sweet-natured insurance man named
Jack Steel. Jack was a bit older, and Bar already had her white

hair, and everybody thought she must be Jack's wife—they used to laugh about that. They laughed about so many things: one man came to the door in his underpants; one woman hawked up a big gob, spat it into the flowerpot; once, the bus lost Bar and Jack, and they sat on a curb under a streetlight till ten o'clock . . . but she loved it. She became a campaigner. It wasn't politics with her—it was just for George. Her attitude was simple: it was anything he wanted to do.

Sometimes, they'd load up the bus and carry the whole show hundreds of miles across the state. They'd carry along a cowboy band, the Black Mountain Boys, who'd draw a crowd that Bush would ply with lemonade . . . and they'd dress up the gals in red, white, and blue, with white skimmer hats that said BUSH BELLES on the bands, and sashes with painted bluebonnets, that read BLUEBONNET BELLES FOR BUSH. Bar made purses for all the Bush Belles with a needlepoint elephant, and BUSH in big white letters. She must have made a hundred—the steady volunteers got handbags, too.

It was mostly volunteers in the big Houston office, an abandoned ballet school in an old loft on Main Street. The place was grungy, but the mirrors on the long walls made it look like there were hundreds of workers. And you couldn't beat the rent . . . or the maintenance: whenever anything broke down—plumbing, air-conditioning . . . happened all the time—instructions were to call George's friend Bake. His daddy owned the building. Bake was a local lawyer—husband of a Bush Belle—James A. Baker III. Aleene Smith came over from the party office, to keep the operation in line. (Anyway, she couldn't have stayed with the party: when George resigned as county chairman, the Birchers took over . . . Kernel Napalm at the helm . . . their first act was to throw out every scrap of paper that mentioned George, or Bush for Senate.)

Houston was the biggest operation in the state. (C. Fred Chambers worked from Houston: he was finance chairman. The Bush family worked from Houston, too: George W.—Junior— seventeen that year, poured his heart into that campaign, all summer.) But Bush also set up a statewide office in the capital, Austin. He wouldn't concede any bit of the state—not the Negro wards of Houston, or Dallas; not even the machine-Democrat Mexican shantytowns of the Rio Grande Valley—why shouldn't the GOP get Latin votes? Why couldn't Bush have friends there, too? . . . In Midland, heart of the oil patch, it seemed the whole town was out for Bush. Two weeks after his announcement, they scheduled a rally, strung a huge BUSH banner right across Wall Street; thirty oil wives and daughters dressed as Bush Belles; they rented the auditorium at San Jacinto Junior High—packed the place! A thousand people came . . . in Midland! George's local chairman, Martin Allday, an old friend, an oil and gas lawyer, did the introducing that night:

"Ladies and gentlemen . . . the only man I have personally known, who I thought should one day be President . . ."

But Bush was a long way from President—even Senator. There were 254 counties in Texas (in an area wider than New York to Chicago; longer than Chicago to Birmingham), and 200 of them never had a real Republican organization. Bush probably worked through half himself, and he had an amazing personal grasp of his affairs: by June '64, when he'd won a plurality in the primary, and beat Jack Cox head to head in a run-off (cleaned his clock: won better than sixty percent!); by the time Martin Allday left his law practice in Midland and moved to Austin to take over campaign management, Bush could run through the state, without any notes, county by county, knew the names of major supporters in each. Problem was, the list wasn't long enough. And by that time, Kennedy was dead, LBJ was President—he'd clobber Goldwater in Texas . . . and his name at the top of the ticket would pull thousands of extra Democrats to the polls, to give their favorite son his own full term in the White House.

Still, Bush was sure he could pull it off. He could feel things changing, everywhere he went. Bush for a Greater Texas! . . . Bush for a Greater America! . . . George Bush was the youth, the future: his brochures showed a bold young man charging into a crowd, his suit coat slung over one shoulder . . . it was the style of "vigor," the style of a Kennedy. And he was sure he knew the people—he made *thousands* of new friends, he could *feel it* . . . they *liked* him! If he could just hang the lib-rull label on Yarborough . . . if he could just show the people that old phony was a *giveaway artist* . . . if he could just attack hard enough, long enough. . . . That was George's method, from the start. That's what state party leaders had *told him to do*: attack, and keep attacking.

Alas, he was not that good on attack. It never seemed natural with him, no matter how many times he did it. The general election was all stump speeches, six to eight a day, with plane or bus trips in between. After weeks of this, Bush had a standard

speech: Sukarno, the UN, foreign aid, taxes, the oil industry
. . . but it never added up to a picture of Bush, or any kind of
message—except Yarborough was too lib-rull. When he'd get
onto Yarborough, Bush's voice would start to climb, his hands
would leap up and slash the air—you couldn't tell where the
hell he was going, except in a general drift to the right. And the
farther right he drifted, the more frantic he became: Bush always
screamed and sawed the air harder when he had to convince
himself that he believed. . . .

Yarborough was *un-Texan!* . . . *left wing!* . . . *selling our state
down the river!* . . . Bush opposed the new Civil Rights Act and
lambasted Yarborough for voting to choke off a filibuster on it
. . . Bush said America ought to get the hell out of the UN, if that
organization seated the Red Chinese . . . Congress ought to cut
off foreign aid if those foreign commie-leaning tinhorns didn't
wanna play ball . . . the United States ought to arm the Cuban
exiles . . . and get *tough* in Vietnam (including use of nuclear
weapons—if that's what the military called for).

But the harder he screamed, the more he played into Yarborough's hands. LBJ was demolishing Goldwater by painting
him as a right-wing extremist, a warmonger, a mad bomber . . .
so Yarborough hopped on board: George Bush, Yarborough said,
was so extreme, so far out in right field . . . (What's that my opponent wants? *The H-bomb?* . . . *in Vitt-namm?*) . . . Why, no
wonder that boy was . . . the darling of the *Birchers!*

The Birchers! George's friends couldn't believe it! You
couldn't get those right-wing nuts to *say* the name Bush . . .
without spitting. But how could you explain that to everyone in

Pecos, or Waco, Brownsville, Texarkana? . . . How could you convince anybody, with George Bush out there, screaming himself hoarse?

Martin Allday, the new campaign manager, had a long talk with George one night, after hearing that stump speech. Maybe Bush should just, you know, try to be more like himself. . . . No, Bush said. He was doing what he had to. He had to attack, if he wanted to win . . . and he could win! He knew he was getting to Yarborough now, with those wild charges the Senator made. And Yarborough refused to debate him. "We got him on the run!" George said. He'd heard old Yarborough speak at a picnic—it was *scandalous*! The man just promised anything he could think of! That's why it was so important, Bush said. We need honest people in government. Honest people, together, can do good things for the country.

Bush wasn't shouting now, and he talked to Martin for a half-hour straight, about what the campaign meant to him. He talked about his father, how he'd served . . . how George felt that's why he was here: to serve . . . and about the notion of duty, courage . . . and what was *right*, what was *right in this country* . . . how it must be protected . . . that's why George had to serve.

And Martin, who loved Bush anyway, was moved: it made him feel *good, clean, excited* to be doing something like this. So he said to Bush:

"Why don't you say *that*? . . ."

"Nah."

That was private stuff.

And C. Fred Chambers heard Yarborough talking about his

war record, so he said to Bush: "Why don't you mention your own service? Give people a feel for your life . . ."

"Nah . . . I'd just feel funny doing that."

He wasn't going to start thumping his chest, let *politics* change the way he was!

And George's brother, Johnny, heard him speak, and suggested a coach. Johnny was an actor—he knew the ropes—he knew a coach who could help. "Just so you can put your point across! . . ."

"Nah."

He wasn't gonna start acting now. He had Yarborough on the run!

He did get under the old man's skin: Yarborough wouldn't debate, so Bush and Allday invented the empty-chair debates. They'd rent a hall and advertise, and when the crowd got settled, they'd bring out Bush, and an empty chair. Then they'd play a tape of Yarborough speaking, and Bush would blast away at him—at his empty chair. Then they'd play another minute of the tape, and Bush would blast away again. It got ink in the papers—always a picture, too. Bush heard Yarborough was so pissed off, he threatened to sue.

But Yarborough never had to call in lawyers. He called in Lyndon, instead. In the homestretch, just as Bush felt he was making his move, pulling even, maybe pulling away (he couldn't be sure—he'd run out of money for polls) . . . LBJ flew back to Texas.

Sure, Lyndon hated Ralph Yarborough. Could not abide the man—said so a hundred times—but hell was gonna freeze over *twice* before he'd let Texas send *two* Republican Senators to Washington. He'd left the state alone for a minute, and for Chrissake got John Tower in *his seat*! This time, he'd keep a hold of the bacon: even if it was Yarborough bacon.

So Lyndon flew in, with the whole White House fanfare . . . and in front of, seemed like, half the cameras in the world, he categorically endorsed Yarborough, he *physically* endorsed Yarborough. Gave him a hug that nearly disappeared him.

Of course, the photo made the front of every paper. This was Lyndon come home! What the hell, this was the *President* . . . which still meant a good big deal in Texas.

Meant a good big deal to George Bush, too. When LBJ flew into Houston to endorse his opponent, Bush called Aleene at the ballet studio on Main Street . . . with instructions:

"I want everybody to go downstairs when the motorcade passes, and wave to the President."

"You gotta be kidding."

"No. Everybody downstairs."

It was a matter of respect—the personal code. He couldn't let politics change something like that.

TWO NIGHTS BEFORE THE end of the campaign, Yarborough went on TV for his last statewide address: there he was, painting Bush into the mad-bomber corner again. He asked his audience: "Doesn't he understand the terrible consequences of the atom bomb? The fallout . . . disease . . . cancer, leukemia?"

George had bought time for the following night. He was having a rubdown at the Houston Club, just before his last speech. Martin Allday stood by the white table, while the masseur worked on Bush's back.

"George? . . ."

"Nggnnnn?"

"You could really hit him in the teeth with that . . . you know, leukemia." Martin was thinking about Robin, the daughter who'd died.

"I know," Bush said. And then, softly: "I'm not gonna bring family . . . bring it up."

So he just went on with the UN . . . taxes . . . lib-rulls—the standard stump. Then he went to his last rally, at the Whitehall Hotel in Houston. You could see it on him like a light from above: George thought he could win. So did the crowd. They loved him like people loved the Kennedys. They were wild for him.

But the next day, LBJ swept the country, and swept Yarborough in behind him. The final count was fifty-six percent for Yarborough, forty-four for Bush. The Latin votes, Negro votes, which Bush had sought all over the state—they went straight-lever Democrat. The Birchers—their precincts went Goldwater, eight-to-two, but they took a walk on the Senate.

At the ballroom Bush had rented for his victory celebration, George W. Bush—Junior—sat with his back to the crowd, in tears. Aleene found him, sat herself down, said: "Can I cry with you?" And she did.

Martin Allday was crushed, couldn't forgive himself ("I just, by God, hurt in the stomach, for the next three weeks").

But George came to the podium late that night, and congratulated the Senator—who, he said, beat him fair and square. He'd looked around, Bush said, for someone to blame . . . and only found himself.

And the next day, George and Bar were in the office, to help clean up. Bar was a little weepy. But George, he'd spent the whole night calling people to thank them . . . and they were so *nice*!

What the hell? He'd got more votes than any Republican in the history of Texas. He said to friends:

"Don't worry. That's only the start."

6

BUSH KNEW HE WAS headed for the Senate. That's where he belonged, like his dad. He had no doubt. He could have held that House seat forever, like a birthright: that new district, Houston's Seventh, had been birthed for him. After one term (in fact, by the filing deadline—after thirteen months on the job), he was unopposed!

And he was a certified star: there were forty new Republicans elected to that Congress, in the rebound after the Goldwater debacle. Bush was chosen as president of the freshman class. For the first time in decades, a GOP freshman got a seat on Ways and Means. (Pres Bush had called on old friends for his son.) From the start, everybody knew about this bright, handsome young Republican . . . from *Houston*—a chink (at last!) in the solid South. George Bush was the party's bold breeze of the future.

He was invited to address GOP luncheons, and breakfasts of bigwigs. He'd talk about the revival of the two-party system— change on the southern wind! What a hopeful vision! He wore that excitement like a suit coat thrown over one shoulder, as he strode down the hallways with a greeting and a grin—he was having such a good time.

It wasn't legislating that ran his motor: he wasn't one of those annoying first-termers who think they've got to make floor speeches and pepper the House with bills. The only bills he pushed were aid for birth control (always an interest of Pres's—maybe unfinished business for the old man) and a short-lived proposal on congressional ethics. (This pup published his tax returns!) . . . Most of his work he did in committee, as a quiet, respectful student of the chairman, Wilbur Mills. (Mills loved him: after the kid filed that birth-control bill, Mills always called him Rubbers.) . . . When the bells rang, Bush would hustle to the floor, check in . . . but most days—just speeches, or conference reports—he could leave with his new friend, the Mississippi Democrat, Sonny Montgomery, for a do-or-die dollar-a-game paddleball match in the House gym.

It was the life itself that Bush found bracing: all the doing, new friends—he was in such demand! There wasn't a minute to sit around: he had committee, he had a lunch, a meeting at Interior! . . . He'd grab his coat and bolt for his office door, calling over his shoulder to Aleene Smith (she'd come with him from Houston): "Allie! See what Mr. Holburn needs, will you—he's on the phone!" . . . He'd *run* through the anteroom, with that lock of hair falling onto his forehead, and the ladies of his office clucking, through their smiles: "Mr. Bush! Tuck in your shirt-tail!"

(In Houston—it was Houston every other weekend, no matter the effort required—the office ladies adored George Bush. Sometimes, if things got slow, Bush would exit his inner office in a flying ballet leap—just to make *les gals* giggle. Late one day, a little woman came by. She was a mousy sort, no makeup, poor dress—probably a hard-luck case. She wanted to see Mr. Bush. But the ladies had no time to tell him before he flew into the office in a twisting *tour jeté*. . . . Then he saw the woman. He froze . . . on the ball of one foot, with his arms outstretched . . . and blushed crimson to the roots of his hair.)

No wonder they loved him—and talked about the way he was: how *a man like that* could be so nice. He'd pick up the phone himself if it rang more than twice, and he'd listen to some voter's tale of woe. ("No," he'd say to the phone. "No, that doesn't sound right, at all. We'll look into it, right away. . . . No! Thank *you* for calling!") Same with the mail: answers by return post. Aleene would cram his battered briefcase every night—might be thirty or forty letters typed up. He'd sign every one, add a couple of lines in his lefty scrawl. The Capitol postman told Aleene that Bush got more mail than anyone else in the Longworth Building. (That's because he sent more. One Houston lady wrote him a letter. So, he wrote her back. So, she wrote to thank him for his response. So, he wrote her back, thanking her for her thank-you note. Finally, she sent him a letter that said: "You remind me of my aunt, Mrs. Ponder. She just won't stay written to.")

This wasn't exactly politics with Bush—more like life. The day his moving van arrived in Washington, it was a terrible snow: George sent Bar off to Sears, through the storm, to buy sheets so the movers could stay the night—he insisted! . . . Don

Rhodes was a volunteer on his campaign in Houston. Rhodes had a hearing problem, and people thought he was strange, maybe slow-witted. (He wasn't.) Bush not only took him along for the Washington staff, he moved Don into his house. . . . Visitors from his district (in fact, visitors from all over Texas; Bush had run statewide before he ever had a district)—George might have asked them to sleep over, too, if he'd had room. As it was, he had to hold himself to fussing over them in the office, posing for pictures, leading tours of the Capitol, making sure they got to see everything in Washington, and . . . wasn't it great how it worked out? Bush inherited a couple of staff ladies from the Texas Democrat who used to represent his part of Houston, so, of course, they knew the crowd in LBJ's White House. They'd call up and get *special* tours: not just the state rooms, but the Family Quarters (that picture of George Hamilton on Lynda Bird's night table!)—well, you put that together with a ride on Bush's *boat* (George just had to show them how the city looked from the Potomac), and Bar's picnic, with the pâté, wine, and salad, and . . . no wonder he was unopposed!

In fact, that was one reason he could make that vote—'68, the open-housing bill—Bush knew he would face no opponent in November. Still, there'd be a howl of protest. Sonny Montgomery told him, in the gym: "Your district ain't gonna like this." Bush didn't need analysis from Sonny. For God's sake, some of Bush's voters wouldn't ride in a car that a Negro had sat in—wouldn't play the same *golf course.* . . . Bush agonized for weeks.

What stuck in his mind was Vietnam, his trip, those

soldiers—black soldiers—in the jungle, in the uniform of their country . . . how could he let them come back to a nation where they couldn't live where they chose? He could not. He couldn't let politics change the way he was.

So he voted for the bill. He meant to take the heat.

But this wasn't heat. This was . . . ugly. First the calls—*les gals* had to hear them:

"You tell Bush we don' need no Connecticut Nigra-lovers . . ."

"Are you half nigger-blood, too? . . ."

Then the letters—thousands of letters. Don Rhodes was up all night trying to get out answers. But how could Bush answer?

"It's Communist says who I can sell my house to . . ."

"I know niggers are running the government . . ."

The threats menaced his staff and his family. One letter mentioned his children by name. After a week, Bush looked like he'd aged ten years. His face sagged. There was no excitement in his words or walk. He went back to Houston, and . . . that was worse. The office felt like the Alamo. The ladies tried to cheer him:

"They're just kooks," Sarah Gee said.

"They aren't thinking . . ."

"Everybody else is for you . . ."

Bush just sat at his desk, staring at the wall. Sarah saw the look of the bereaved. She didn't even know why she said it—it just came out:

"Oh, George . . . I'm sorry."

Bob Mosbacher called, said the moneymen were up in arms. "You want me to try to get 'em together, talk to them?"

Bush's voice was weary:

"No, I gotta do it myself."

So, he did: he got twenty-five big givers into a room. Bush had the air of a man who'd been beat up. "I know we agree on so *much*," he told them. He didn't ask them to support his vote— just to keep in mind the other votes. It was almost pleading! "If you can't support me anymore . . . well, I hope I can still have your friendship."

He did feel he was beaten—not this time, no, it was too late to lose reelection . . . but what about next time? What about the Senate? All the great doings, the big plans ahead? . . . In fact, his loss went deeper than elections: it had to do with the choices he'd made for twenty years—in Texas—his feeling that he could speak for Texas. Was he wrong? . . . God! What if it was *all wrong?*

He wrote to a friend:

"I never dreamed the reaction would be so violent. Seething hatred—the epithets—the real chickenshit stuff in spades—to our [office] girls: 'You must be a nigger or a Chinaman'—and on and on—and the country club crowd disowning me and denouncing me. . . .

"Tonight [I was on] this plane and this older lady came up to me. She said, 'I'm a conservative Democrat from this district, but I'm proud, and will always vote for you now'—and her accent was Texan (not Connecticut) and suddenly somehow I felt that maybe it would all be OK—and I started to cry—with the poor lady embarrassed to death—I couldn't say a word to her."

He would always remember the moment when he knew . . .

that night—a town meeting. The crowd booed him and muttered his name with a menacing hiss as he was introduced.

So he told them, he knew what they thought. He told them, he knew some people called him lib-rull. But it wasn't conservative or liberal—this vote. It was just . . . fairness. He told them about Vietnam—those soldiers—how could he let them come back? . . . How could you slam a door in a guy's face, just 'cause he's a Negro, or speaks with an accent? . . .

There was no more to say. He was going to sit down, in the silence. He turned to thank the moderator, and behind him he heard applause, a scattered few, and then, when he turned, more clapping, everybody was clapping . . . and then some stood, in front, and more behind. They were clapping—*for him*—because he did what he thought was right, and he'd said so. He didn't think they agreed—still—but they gave him a standing ovation.

God! He could have kissed them all!

THAT'S HOW HE KNEW, he was going to the Senate—not a doubt. This time, 1970, he would beat old Yarborough fair and square—he *knew* it—Texas was changing!

That's what Bush kept saying: Yarborough was out of touch! The state had passed him by. People didn't want that New Deal, promise-'em-the-moon kind of government, that kind of Senator—no. They wanted a modern conservative. They wanted George Bush!

This time, he'd have his ducks in a row. He'd been around,

he had friends everywhere. This time, he'd have a professional campaign manager—Marvin Collins, great guy! He was signed on already. He'd have a big budget—two million, for starters. And a Bush-friend, John Tower, had taken over the Republican Senatorial Campaign Committee—he'd send along whatever he could. And the President would help! President Nixon was on a roll: he was targeting races all over the country. Nixon said Texas was number one, and he asked Bush to run—personally! Even LBJ might help. Bush went to see him. The old man certainly wouldn't lift a finger to help Yarborough. Neither would John Connally. They all hated Ralph! . . . This time, Bush wouldn't have to scrape for issues—he'd had his eye on Yarborough for six years. He had the old snake-oil salesman locked in the crosshairs.

Bush had such big plans for 1970: ads all over the state, and not just in cities, but on every dustland radio station—Spanish, too! Bush didn't see why this race, his race, should not mark the *realignment* of Texas. Why shouldn't the GOP grab its share of the Mexicans? And Negroes—my God, he *ought* to get some Negro votes! (Election night, 1968, though he had no contest, he'd *grabbed* for the tally sheets: he wanted to see those colored precincts. Wouldn't you know it? Jeez! . . . After all that— two-thirds wouldn't even cross over for him—with *no Democrat against him*!) . . . But that wouldn't matter—that would be gravy—once he started hammering away at the old guard, the liberal, the tired voice of the past, Yarborough.

Then, the unthinkable happened: with a vicious, attacking campaign, a south Texas Democrat, a businessman (and former

Rep) named Lloyd Bentsen . . . came out of *nowhere* (actually, he came out of Connally's hip pocket) . . . and took the senior Senator down. Yarborough lost his primary. George Bush lost his target.

Now it was Bush against Bentsen—and all of Bush's plans were air. George tried to tell folks it was fine—this would be *easier*—but even his friends couldn't see it. Bentsen was conservative—just like Bush, when you got down to it—and tough (he proved *that* against old Ralph). Bentsen could play the veteran card (he was a pilot in the war, too) and the business card (he'd made more of a pile than Bush). He had the same congressional experience as Bush. He was just as nasty on Crime 'n' Commies, a practiced south Texas hand with the Mexicans, a Democrat Texans could live with. . . . So, here came Lyndon's pals from the Perdenales . . . and here came that greazy John Connally on the tube, making ads for Bentsen . . . here came all the courthouse Dems, the yellow-dog Dems, and the better-dead-than-red Dems. Bentsen brought them all back from the grave. Worse still, here came a ballot issue to allow sale of liquor by the drink. So thousands of rural Baptists would turn out against demon rum . . . and on the way, they'd likely vote the standard Democrat ticket.

And Bush? Well, he had the Republicans—but there still weren't many of those. (The electorate was at least four-to-one Democratic). . . . He had his friends in business, his constituents in Houston. . . . His manager, Marvin Collins, tried to cook a deal with the liberal Democrats (who hated Bentsen for what he'd done to Yarborough), and he nurtured a noisy group of

Democrats for Bush. . . . Bush still had high hopes for the Negro vote. He'd gone to the *wall* for those people!

That was half the problem. Everybody knew about his open-housing vote—Bentsen made sure of that. And about that time Bush had voted for the *Yeww Ennn*! Bentsen brought that up, too. . . . In fact, Bentsen ran close enough to the right-field wall, there was no way Bush could get outside of him. . . . Bush was the, uh, *lib-rull*!

Still, Bush was *sure* he could pull it out. People liked him! He had so many friends! He was working so hard! . . . Bush still thought he could cast the race as the Democratic past against the future. "We're on the threshold," he'd scream in every speech, "of a new de-*cade*!" (No one had the heart to tell him that Texans didn't accent that second syllable. He was working *so* hard—they didn't want to hurt him.) . . . If he could just show *he was* that future, that vigor, that youth. (With those kids rounded up by his Youth Coordinator, Rob Mosbacher, and Junior Bush, who'd cut away, when he could, from his National Guard flight training, the Bush campaign had the look of a Scout trip.) . . . If Bush could show, somehow, that Bentsen was just another page from the past . . .

But that was the other half of the problem: Bentsen didn't seem to have any past—not like Yarborough, not a past they could use. They dug up Bentsen's votes from Congress, but that was stuff from the *forties*, no one would give a damn. Oh, there was one guy came in with a tip—said it would *finish* Bentsen. Bush sent Aleene to the Ag Department in Washington. She sat there all day, writing down the information (with a couple of department lawyers at her elbow, clucking about how she might *embarrass* a former *Secretary*—most unfortunate!). . . . But when she brought the poop to Bush, he read the file and just shook his head: he wasn't going to be that way about politics. No, he could only be what he was.

That's how the problems started with Nixon. The President got it into his mind that George Bush *would not go for the kill.* . . . Nixon sent money—more than a hundred thousand dollars from one of his illegal slush funds . . . but Bush wouldn't use it to take Bentsen down. The White House offered to send Tricia Nixon, David Eisenhower . . . or surrogates who'd throw *red meat* to the press—bring in the tough guys. How about that Bob Dole? . . . Or Spiggy Agnew? . . .

Bush didn't want them . . . but when it got to Agnew, he could not say no: the Vice President of the United States! So Agnew came, and then Nixon himself. How could Bush say no to the President? . . . And in the last days of the campaign, both made blistering partisan speeches—wiped out any hope Bush had with Democrats.

On election night, family and friends gathered at the old Shamrock Hotel. Bush knew it would be tight—his last polls showed the race even. But he *knew* he could win—good things happen to good people. He had to believe. The family was in a suite—upstairs from the big ballroom, with the band, balloons, and streamers. George and Bar were on a couch: his arms around Doro and Marvin, Bar holding Neil and Jebbie. They turned on the TV, and . . . it was over. *Twelve minutes* into the broadcast— after two years of work (*seven* years, since he started for that seat)—Walter Cronkite said his computers called the race for Bentsen. Doro started crying. Marvin Bush started crying. George Bush hugged them, told them it would be all right. Neil and Jebbie cried in Bar's arms. The friends started crying. Aleene was sobbing. Sarah Gee started cursing the nuts. Nancy Crouch said she was through with politics. Marvin Collins felt like he'd been hit by a car. He went off to Junior Bush's apartment, and those two stayed teary till they were too blotto to care.

The one who didn't cry was George Bush. He went around the suite, telling everyone what a great job they'd done. Then he was on the phone. "Well," he'd say, "back to the drawing board." Downstairs, in the ballroom, he conceded, then stayed for an hour, answering anything the press had to ask. Then he was back on the phone . . . all night. At five A.M., he pulled out a list— hundreds of people he wanted to thank, and he started from the top. He'd be on the phone for sixteen hours straight. Bar couldn't sit there and watch—couldn't bear that, couldn't chip in, brightly, like she had in '64: "Well, there'll be another time." . . . No, 1970 was different. George Bush had run for the Senate twice, and lost—could there be another time? She went off with her girlfriends to the club: a tennis game, her doubles . . . but she was standing at the net and kept thinking of George, on his phone, trying to cheer people, telling them they'd done *so well* . . . and her eyes blurred with tears and she couldn't even see the ball . . . she felt the hand of a friend on her shoulder, and a voice:

"Oh, the hell with this, Bar. Let's go in and have a martini."

So they did. They may have had several.

7

Bar told him not to take that job. "Anything . . . but not that committee."

It was the first time she'd ever said something like that, but . . . the Republican National Committee? It was . . . just *politics*, just thumping the old tub! . . . Oh, she'd been to enough of those dinners to know the score. Bob Dole could run around the country, saying nasty things about the Democrats—fine . . . but that was a *lousy* job for George Bush! . . . George Bush was serving the country!

They'd been happy in New York, at the UN—in their grand apartment in the Waldorf (actually three apartments put together, on the forty-second floor of the Towers). After all those terrible things people wrote (she remembered well) when George got the job: how he was "just a politician," "ignorant of foreign affairs," who would "devalue the U.S. mission," whose appointment "demonstrated Nixon's contempt"—George had shown them, hadn't he?

119

He was a raging success . . . he'd done his homework, he knew the issues. He'd represented his country with honor. The staff at the mission loved him—as did the foreign diplomats, whom the Bushes entertained assiduously, with dinners in New York, picnics at his mother's place in Greenwich, nights at the ballpark to watch Uncle Herbie's Mets—George had made so many friends! . . . Actually, George and Bar had, since she got hold of a Blue Book, the list of diplomats and their wives—she memorized the names, made sure to talk to them all, at parties . . . then she'd take them over and introduce them to George— they made a wonderful team.

Bar would bring her needlepoint and sit through Security Council debates. She tried not to sit next to the wife of someone George would vote against—but if it happened, no matter: they could still be friends. After all, they were professionals. They had to take the line of their governments. Everybody understood that—understood there could be no deviation from that, no matter what one might think privately. In fact, there was no job (none in Bar's experience) where the power of mind-set came in so handy. No one but Bar knew when George had argued for a different policy in Washington. (It happened seldom, as a matter of fact.) But George would *never* sow discord within his delegation, and he wouldn't allow any carping about the State Department, or Secretary of State Kissinger. No one but Bar would see Bush's heartache when he picked up the paper and found out Henry Kissinger was secretly talking with the Red Chinese—pulled the rug out from under Taiwan . . . and from under George Bush, who was laboring to keep Taiwan in the

UN. . . . No, Bush would simply take the *new line*—a two-China policy—no one would *ever* see him acting as if he did not believe it. . . . No one but Bar would ever know his humiliation and rage when the United States lost the vote on two Chinas, and the Third World delegates ("little wiener nations," Bush had called them) started laughing and whooping, catcalling Uncle Sam, in the aisles. . . . No, he would gather the delegation and reassure them: they were a good team—no second-guessing and no looking back . . . "On to the next event!"

That was the loyalty he owed to his country—and his President. Richard Nixon had vouchsafed this job to Bush, after Bush lost his race for the Senate. No one would ever see Bush wavering from Richard Nixon. That's why the hard-eyed men in the White House thought of Bush for that RNC job. ("He takes our line beautifully," said a memo from Bob Haldeman.) And that's why Barbara Bush could hardly have been surprised when loyal George came back from Camp David and gave her the news she least wanted to hear. . . . Actually, he didn't have to tell her, straight out.

"Boy!" said George Bush. "You just can't say no to the President!"

Thank you for your note about the Watergate affair. I want to say I left the wonderful job at the United Nations to return to politics because I feel strongly that those of us who care must try to elevate politics.

The connotations of Watergate are grubby and I don't like it. . . . There is a public distrust in government and to

the degree that I can make some small contribution to cor-
recting that, this new job in politics will be worthwhile.
I appreciate your taking the time to write . . .

Yours very truly,
George Bush

He answered each letter personally, assuring Republicans
that their party had nothing to do with Watergate, promising
the faithful that he'd spare no effort to trumpet the President's
achievements, adjuring the Nixon-haters not to judge too soon or
too harshly—to let the constitutional process take its course. . . .
What else could he do? He told his friends—the ones who counseled him to get off that sinking ship—that he wasn't just defending the President, he was defending the party, and the Presidency.

I fully share your concern about this sordid and grubby
Watergate mess. . . .
Watergate was the product of the actions of a few mis-
guided, very irresponsible individuals who violated a high
trust and who served neither the President nor their country
well. . . .
Keep in mind that the RNC and CRP are two separate
entities. The whole Party shouldn't be blamed for the ac-
tions of a few zealots. . . .

Yours very truly,
George Bush

But he was defending the President—no way around it. Richard Nixon had assured Bush, personally, that he had nothing to do with the break-in, the cover-up—any of that nonsense. . . . Bush had the President's *word*—man to man.

And how could he demonstrate his continued belief in the man who had become his friend, his patron . . . save by throwing himself into defense—personally? Bush knew no other way.

> *The President has said repeatedly he wasn't involved in the sordid Watergate affairs. I believe him. I am confident he will be fully exonerated once this matter is cleared up in the courts.*
>
> *I am also confident that people are basically fair. . . . The voters will not hold the Republicans responsible for what the Party was not involved in. . . .*
>
> *Yours very truly,*
> *George Bush*

If Bush was confident, he was more and more alone. Yale friends wrote, asking why he could not *do something* to rid the country of Nixon. Republican officials relayed forecasts of disaster in elections to come. Money for the Party disappeared. Bush had to fire half the staff at the committee. He handled each termination personally.

When GOP Congressmen edged toward impeachment, or Senators mused on Nixon's possible resignation . . . Bush's phone would ring. The White House was on the line—Chuck Colson, or one of his legion (Bob Teeter, the party pollster, called them "the after-dark crowd"). . . .

"YOU GO OUT THERE AND TELL THOSE ASSHOLES . . ."

You could hear Colson's snarl in Bush's earpiece, all the way across the office.

". . . THEY FUCK WITH US, WE'LL CRUSH 'EM . . . LIKE BUGS! ALL OF 'EM . . ."

And you'd see Bush's back go stiff, in his big chair, as he said with conscious quiet to the phone: "I'm not sure that would do any good . . . I'm not sure that's what the committee ought to be doing."

Then there'd be more of Colson, screaming . . . after which, Bush would set down the earpiece in its cradle, precisely, almost daintily, with thumb and index finger pincering its midpoint, only the tips of two fingers touching it. . . . "Well," he'd say, "that was pleasant."

. . . I have read every word of the transcripts, but I have not seen all the evidence, and thus, I am not going to join in suggesting that Richard Nixon authorized payment of hush money. Indeed, I am surprised that one who is concerned about government as you would not understand the point that all evidence should be seen and heard before definitive judgments are made by Members of Congress.

Yours very truly,
George Bush

. . . I recognize that it is very hard to get the message of support out around the country, particularly when the press is having such a heyday with Watergate and the negative aspects.

> Yours very truly,
> George Bush

. . . Last year for example, I traveled 97,000 miles, to 33 states, gave 101 speeches, 78 press conferences, was on national TV 11 times to speak for Nixon. . . .
We really need you.

> Yours very truly,
> George Bush

No, it could not be just letters, or phone calls. Bush flew around the nation with abandon, interposing his person between the Republican Party and its date with a brick wall. The speeches and press statements were the same as the letters—same words—but Bush thought if people could *see him, hear him, in person* . . . see his hope for the nation, for its government, for his party, its candidates, for *decency* . . . well, that would make a difference—wouldn't it?

That was what he had to give, that was the measure of loyalty—and the requirement of the code: personal commitment.

That's what made it worse, in the end . . . when he found out. Nixon had lied to him, personally.

Bush never could shrug that off—couldn't chalk it up to politics . . . that wasn't politics to *him*. That was a personal breach.

Even a year later, Bush remarked to a friend, with uncharacteristic bluntness: "I wouldn't care if I never see Richard Nixon again."

Of course, by that time, Bush had less reason to be politic. In fact, he wasn't sure whether politics was his game, at all.

GEORGE BUSH THOUGHT HE deserved some consideration, some future. God knows, he'd paid his dues. Everywhere he went, there were people who thought he was mixed up in that mess— people couldn't keep all the names straight—Haldeman, Colson . . . Ehrlichman, Dean, Stans, Butterfield . . . Bush! . . . But that was over, thank God.

Ford was President now. Ford was a friend.

Gerald Ford had to pick a Vice President.

This wasn't something Bush dreamed up. He was encouraged to consider the job. People who were close to the President—very close—told him . . . no guarantees, but everyone agreed it made sense. George Bush had friends in a hundred nations, from his days at the UN . . . friends all over the country from his term at the RNC—state committeemen, county chairmen . . . friends in Congress, strength in Texas—he could help Ford all across the South . . . he was a seasoned pol, but just a month or two out of his forties—Bush was the future of the party. He'd make a hell of a Veep!

In fact, this wasn't the first time Bush had been considered. Back in '68 his name had come up, when Nixon got the nomination in Miami. Bush's friend, Dick Moore, brought the name up at a meeting . . . but Bush was only a first-term Rep; Nixon thought he needed seasoning.

In '73, when Agnew copped a plea in a Baltimore courtroom, Dick Moore was once again at Nixon's side. . . . What about George Bush? Hell of a guy! Hell of a résumé! . . . Nixon thought Bush wasn't tough enough. Nice fellow—Nixon always liked his dad—but George was, maybe, too nice (not "one of us" to Nixon and his crowd), an Ivy Leaguer, through and through. Nixon was so surprised to hear that Bush was captain of the Yale ball team! . . . Really? *Bush?*

Anyway, Nixon took Jerry Ford . . . but things worked out for Bush. *Now* . . . his time had come. Good things happen to good people. Loyalty and patience could not fail to bring rewards.

Not that Bush was going to lie back, let nature run its course . . . no. He did what he could:

From the chairmanship of the RNC, it was an easy matter to poll the national committee (just for the President's information, understand).

Behold! The favorite, nationwide, of Republican Committeemen and women was . . . George Bush!

Then he arranged for a poll of Republican members of Congress. Who would they choose for Veep?

George Bush!

From the Oval Office, it had to look like a groundswell: all those people, letters, telegrams—Republicans, all over the country, talking up Bush! . . . Actually, Bush had a friend, a Committeeman from Omaha, Dick Herman, who moved into Washington's Statler Hilton, whence he ran a telephone boiler room, beating the tom-toms for Bush.

At last, in Kennebunkport, Bush got the call: White House on the line! The President had made his decision. . . . The new Vice President of the United States would be . . . Nelson Rockefeller.

Bush was hurt, then angry. What did a guy have to do? He'd stood up—taken heat, put his own good name on the line—through the worst shit-storm his Party ever faced.

What did it get him?

Ford said they'd have to get together soon "to discuss the future."

Goddammit, there'd better be some discussion—because George Bush was through with the RNC.

WELL, FORD COULDN'T HAVE been nicer, more solicitous—after the fact, of course. He said there were two *top-notch* diplomatic posts (Ambassador was still the title Bush used in Washington)—Paris or London . . . Bush could have his pick.

Bush had another idea—China.

China?

It wasn't even an embassy! Just a "listening post." Anyway, China policy was mapped and made by one man—Henry Kissinger. The Liaison Office in Peking had nothing to do. It was there simply to be there. "You'll be bored beyond belief," Kissinger said.

No, Bush was sure it would be *a wonderful adventure* (he and Bar had decided). China was exotic. China was important! China was . . . his choice.

See, you had to look at it as Bush did—that is, through the woeful misadventures of four years.

Here was a young up-and-comer who'd given up his safe House seat to run for the Senate. The President had asked him—and Bush so much wanted into the big game . . . but he caught that bad break with Bentsen . . . and that dream was dashed.

So he went to the UN—but not before he made sure he'd have a seat at the table, Cabinet rank, and the President's ear. "No problem!" the President's men assured him. . . . But in New York, he found he wasn't in the game at all. Nixon and Kissinger were the whole team.

So, loyally, he took the RNC job—making sure he'd keep his seat at the Cabinet table, and *this time* (for sure!) he'd be a player on the President's team . . . But by that time, the captain was about to be drummed out of the league, and the badge of team membership was a public shame.

The loss of the Vice Presidency was just the last straw.

So, China was important . . . enough. China was intriguing . . . enough. China, best of all, was seven thousand miles away.

When he got established in Peking, he wrote to a friend: the warnings were true—there wasn't any work. "So I'm trying to do this job, and meanwhile figure out what I'm going to do with my life."

Bush felt he'd played the game—as hard as he could. Maybe it wasn't the game for him.

⁂

BARBARA BUSH WAS IN love with China. It was her first trip overseas . . . such a wonderful adventure! There was the compound in Peking—a small building for the office, a larger house behind: first floor given over to reception rooms and a spacious dining room; family quarters above—quite cozy. . . . There was a house staff of six (so *interesting*, with their Chinese ways, and strange Maoist stringencies) . . . and a tennis court (with a Chinese pro), where she and George could team up for mixed doubles. . . . There was a new community of foreign diplomats to woo and watch: receptions, reciprocal dinners, national days (such a grand and festive barbecue she and George mounted for July Fourth—the Chinese had never seen anything like it). . . . There were visitors, occasional trips; wonderful food (their head cook, Mr. Sun, was an artist); lots of letters to the kids, who stayed at school in the States. There was an early-model VCR, with tapes of *M*A*S*H* from a friend at CBS. There were daily lessons in Chinese (Bar picked up more than George) and three thousand years of history to learn. There were her bike rides through Peking, to ancient tombs, into strange corners of the city—with friends, or alone, or, best of all, with George.

That was the great thing. Bar had moved into too many different houses (this one in Peking was her twenty-fifth) to fall in love with another pile of brick; staff she'd had, and would have more; new friends—there were always new friends. But in Peking, for the first time since Odessa, Texas (maybe the first time in her married life), she had George Bush to herself. He had no work in the evenings—often none in the afternoons. There were no long cables to write back to Washington, describing his contacts with the Chinese government. Save when Kissinger came to town (twice in their yearlong sojourn), there were no serious contacts with the government . . . unless you counted the tennis pro.

So Bar and George did everything together. They'd pedal off, side by side, in the afternoons, on their way to the Ming tombs, or the Forbidden City, with George waving and smiling to the Chinese on the streets. . . . *"Ni how!"* he'd call, through a gap-mouthed grin. That was Chinese for "How are ya?" . . . except with Bush, sometimes it came out like an indeterminate rodeo whoop. Anyway, if anyone really answered, they'd soon exhaust Bush's stock of Chinese words. But still, they had to come away with a sense of his freshness, his eagerness to know them. What he brought to the historic reopening of U.S. relations with one billion Chinese was the same gift that carried him through every job—his person.

And no one enjoyed that person more than Bar. She was never happier. "I think it's great," she told one friend, "to have a new life every ten years or so." She called China "a whole new leaf in both our lives . . ."

But it was not altogether a new leaf for George—or, he hadn't quite finished turning the old one. In November '75, he got a cable from Kissinger: THE PRESIDENT ASKS THAT YOU CON-

SENT TO HIS NOMINATING YOU AS THE NEW DIREC-
TOR OF THE CENTRAL INTELLIGENCE AGENCY.

Bar said: "I remember Camp David . . ."

What she meant was, she remembered that day, at Camp
David, when George accepted the worst job of his life—the
RNC. What she meant was, the CIA was under the same sort
of cloud as the Nixon campaign of '72. Senator Frank Church's
Select Committee on Intelligence was turning up evidence of
illegal operations, assassination plots, domestic spying. (What
did they know? When did they know it?) . . . She just wanted
George to stop and think: Did he want to walk into another
swamp?

But she had no illusions; George would never refuse the
President. Anyway, she could see how he felt: this was a big job
. . . worldwide . . . critical to the country, critical to the man in
the Oval Office. He wouldn't have to fight for the President's
ear—would he? . . . He cabled back to make sure.

No, he'd have full access, control of his own shop, his own
staff. (Bush started calling himself Head Spook.)

And, within days, he found out that this—that he—was part
of a major shake-up: a new Defense Secretary, Don Rumsfeld;
a new National Security Adviser, Brent Scowcroft; a new Commerce Secretary, Elliot Richardson . . . and most intriguing—a
new opening for the national ticket, in 1976 . . . Nelson Rockefeller had bowed out as Ford's running mate.

Who could tell what would happen now?

There was a whole new team taking the field . . . and, at last,
Bush would be in the great game!

He cabled his acceptance. He flew back to Washington.

Only weeks later did he learn that some Senators (and not just Democrats) didn't want Bush in the game. Only then did he hear the theory (it had occurred to him, as a matter of fact) that they'd brought him back just to smear him in another swamp of misfeasance . . . to give him a job from which he'd *never* recover—not politically, not in the public mind . . . that they'd brought him back to *bury him forever.* Worse still, as the price of his confirmation, they wanted him to remove his name from consideration as Ford's running mate.

How *dare* they? It was like taking away his right to *vote!* It was . . . unconstitutional! Had to be!

Well, maybe. But the decision was out of his hands. Before the Senate Armed Services Committee confirmed Bush's nomination, Gerald Ford wrote a letter, assuring the committee: ". . . There should be continuity in the CIA leadership. Therefore, if Ambassador Bush is confirmed by the Senate as Director of Central Intelligence, I will not consider him as my Vice Presidential running mate in 1976."

8

It seemed always to happen for Bush—the Blessed Confluence. He just tried to be a friend, and it worked out. Even he couldn't understand why. But that's the way it worked in the five-minute devotions, homilies on how the good life is lived, which Dottie Bush read to her children, every day at breakfast.

Good things happen to good people. It was one of those truths he'd just always known.

Much later, when he was grown up, a millionaire man of the world, Bush heard the same lesson from his own minister. The Reverend James T. (Tom) Bagby, rector of St. Martin's Episcopal, in Houston, had a homily he'd tell in church, a lesson from his own life. . . . When Tom was going to seminary, the bishop awarded him one-third of a scholarship, the gift of a wealthy and gracious lady. That year, Tom wrote her a letter every month. The next year, the lady instructed the bishop that Tom was to get the whole scholarship. Why, the bishop asked her, did she want to give the full amount to a student so undistinguished? Reverend Tom always concluded: "Perhaps it's because I did what my mother taught me. Expressing my gratitude was the very least I could have done. . . . Large rewards come from planting small seeds of gratitude."

Lord knows, George Bush had strewn the ground with seeds.

That was the reason for the Christmas cards, at least at the start: a way for George and Bar to keep beaming the glow to the folks they'd left back East, when they moved to Texas. But the way those two were about friends, the list just kept growing. Every year George Bush was alive on the planet, there were more friends to take care of. And the way Bar kept her file cards, no one ever dropped off the list. Bar moved her box of file cards from Midland to Houston, to Washington, back to Houston, to New York, back to Washington, to China, back to Washington, then back to Houston, and to Washington again. Of course, every year it grew, from family and schoolmates, to oil-business friends and new Texas neighbors, and Texas pols, to Washington friends and neighbors, fellow congressmen, then UN Ambassadors from all over the world, and then local pols from all over the country, and more new neighbors, and Chinese officials, and CIA colleagues and foreign intelligence pooh-bahs, and more pols, now from all fifty states and a few from the U.S. territories, and campaign contributors, and volunteers, and staff, and ex-staff, and that wounded soldier he met at the VA, and that lady who told him *such a sad story* at the shopping center in Waco, Texas, and the cop who used to stop traffic every afternoon, as George Bush nosed his car out of the Houston Club garage. Some of the older entries were written over a dozen times for that friend's successive new houses, amended for that family's every new child, and when a child moved away from home, that child got a new file card. By the mid-seventies, say, while the Bushes sojourned in China, Bar had four or five thousand file cards, all updated by year-round effort, stored in a gleaming wooden four-drawer case that held pride of place, like the Roman gods of the household, in the upstairs family room of the residence of the U.S. compound in Peking. Bar used to point it out to guests, as one might mention a family heirloom. One visitor who saw it protested: "Some of those must be just political friends."

And Bar's eyes turned icy as she snapped: "What's the difference? A friend is a friend."

HE HAD LIKED THOSE odds, starting out . . . back in '77, '78. His name recognition stood at zero-point-three percent. One in 333 voters knew Bush's name. His three staff kids (Jim Baker hadn't even come aboard—he was running, unsuccessfully, for attorney general of Texas) would, in time, call themselves the Asterisk Club: Bush was an asterisk in every poll.

The campaign . . . well, they called the 1980 campaign "George Bush's two thousand closest friends." That was the major asset. But Bush had his Christmas card list, his politician friends from the RNC days, his business friends—quite generous with money—and his school friends. That turned into money, too. Bush had been chairman of Campaign for Yale, an ambitious reendowment of Old Blue, which, by degrees, became Campaign for Bush.

And he had one other asset: Jimmy Carter. It was Carter who gave Bush his reason for running—not to mention the time. Bush went to Carter, close of the '76 campaign, and offered to stay on at the CIA. He offered his service—let Carter send a message of bipartisanship . . . Bush would finish the job he had started a year before: restoring the CIA to its proper standing—*above politics.* . . . Carter could have sent a strong signal with that move, but he never really considered it—didn't understand.

Bush was more and more convinced: Carter couldn't see the big picture. Carter was going to be a disaster. Bush had briefed him during the campaign. Once Carter became the nominee, he was entitled to the precious awareness—so Director Bush tried to bring him up to speed: the latest from the listening posts, the poop on the new satellites . . .

"What's the angle on that gimbal? . . ."

"Excuse me?"

"What's the angle on that camera gimbal on the new satellite? What's the *maximum angle?* . . ."

"Uh . . . we'll check on that."

Who the hell cared what's the angle on the GIMBAL? . . . The point was: What can we see? . . . What about forty-five Russian divisions on the *Chinese border?* . . . Can we see if they're *moving?*

To Bush, Carter would ever be a small-time, liberal Governor from Georgia . . . who didn't have a clue to how the world really worked, who was going to . . . *screw . . . everything . . . up.*

So even as Bush drove Bar's Volvo back to Houston . . . as she settled them into another new house . . . as George got on a bank board, started talking up his business career . . . he started turning over the big question:

Could he knock Carter off? . . . Could he get there?

Bush was pretty well convinced that by 1980, voters wouldn't be in the mood to sit through another four years of outsiders, men who didn't know the levers, who ran against Washington. No more Carter—he'd bet on that . . . and maybe no Ronald Reagan. Everyone said Reagan had the 1980 nomination sewed up, after his near miss against Ford, in '76 . . . Bush didn't believe it. Reagan was old hat—and old: Bush would *relish* running that man's aged ass into the ground.

He talked it over with Jim Baker . . . Bake thought they might do it like Carter—work the grassroots in Iowa, establish themselves with a respectable second place as the sensible alternative to Reagan, then burst through (somewhere) with a winner's grin, into the glare.

Candidates in a half-dozen states were already asking Bush to speak—help them out in '78. . . . In an office next to his own in the Citizen's National Bank, Bush set up a PAC to handle the requests, the schedule, the money. That much was fine—he could stop with that . . . or go whole hog.

But could he get there? (Zero-point-three percent!)

He could make a career in business. The bank board, Eli Lilly's board, Purolator, Inc. . . . that came easy to him.

Bar was so much happier since he'd left a job he couldn't talk about—not even to her. She'd felt so left out.

The new house was fine. Houston was homey. He'd drive himself to the bank in the morning, then Don Rhodes would pick him up in his truck, if Bush had a meeting, or a date somewhere.

Wasn't it great how it worked out?

They were in Rhodesy's pickup, spring of '78, on their way to the Ramada Club—Bush had a lunch date.

"Don, I've really gotta decide if I want to run for President."

Rhodes was driving—didn't even turn his head.

"Run," he said. "Y'don't have anything better to do."

THE GREAT THING ABOUT that 1980 campaign was how personal it was. Bush didn't have to work with strangers. Of course, with Bush, no one stayed a stranger for long . . . but for most of those two years, you could meet the whole staff in one weekend hop from Houston to Iowa, and on to New Hampshire.

As for those few select, the Bushies of '78–'79, they were spoiled by all the time spent with him, his endless personal attention. They'd travel with him—Bush and one body man, maybe a local who'd pick them up at the airport. Or, if they weren't along for the ride, there'd be calls from him, every day . . . a personal note if he got ten minutes . . . an invite to burgers and bloodies in the backyard, if he happened to catch a Sunday home in Houston.

There were few days home. In his first year of campaigning, he traveled 180,000 miles, mostly flying coach. After that, the pace picked up. The normal road crew was Bush and David Bates, a twenty-seven-year-old Houston lawyer and body man—child of Bush-friends, childhood friend to Bush-son Jeb—and possessor of a hypereager sunniness that made him seem like a young copy of Ambassador Bush. Bates would show up, early A.M., at the new Bush house on Indian Trail. Don Rhodes would come by with the truck—they'd throw their bags into the bed. By nine in the morning, they'd be in the air to some midday event—Fred Jones for Congress, say—and after Bush told the crowd what a splendid friend was Fred Jones, he'd do a little press conference, if any reporters could be cajoled to hang around. Then came the heavy lifting—private meetings: party leaders, activists, moneymen . . . one-on-one, twenty minutes apiece, for as many hours as it took.

"How's Janey? The kids? . . . Jeez! College already!" (Bush had the names from his travels for the RNC.)

"Listen . . . I really think I've got a good shot at this thing—think I can *win*, and, uh, if you could help, I'd really love to have you on the team."

Some wanted to know how Bush thought he could win . . . and he was ready for that:

"I think I can make a more *active* campaign than Reagan" (i.e., that guy is *ancient*). . . . "I can show I have more experience than Reagan." (Guy doesn't know where the Treasury Department *is*, for God's sake!)

Then they'd ask: Who would he have for State Chairman? Bush was always ready to discuss local politics. He could reel off the names of his supporters in the state without notes, without pause—like some people always know how much money's in their wallet.

Sometimes, a meeting would wind up with the pooh-bah telling Bush: "George, you know I wish you the best . . . but I'd like to give it some thought." Some would say, "Well, George, I know you're going to do well, but I'm committed . . ." (to Dole, John Anderson, Howard Baker, or, usually, Reagan).

Bush always understood if they were committed to somebody else. But if they said they were with him, and didn't come through, they were off the list. That was a breach of the code. The ones that really got to him were the friends who didn't sign up. What did friendship mean, if they weren't going to help?

Whatever they said, Bush would follow up with a note. That's how he spent his time on his afternoon flights: handwritten notes to the one-on-ones. "Really enjoyed the chance to catch up . . . sitting down with you . . . just want to reiterate that I'd really like to have you along." So, if they ever fell off the Reagan boat . . . or when Dole, Baker, or Connally foundered . . . well, those pooh-bahs had a *relationship* with George Bush. Meanwhile, word got around that Bush was working hard, making friends.

That he was: there were also notes to Fred Jones ("Great to see you again . . ."), to the chairman of the Fred Jones event ("Thanks for having me . . ."), to the guy who herded the local press toward Bush, to the drivers, the cooks, the waiter who brought an extra glass of water. . . . Those would be carried back and typed in Houston. Meanwhile, Bush was on his way to a dinner of the World Affairs Council in Indianapolis, or the Rotary in Keene, New Hampshire, or the Chamber of Commerce in . . . well, he did the Chamber everywhere.

Actually, the schedule was more of a bitch than it had to be, because Bush would never say no to a friend. Bates learned to say no by reflex, right away. Margaret Tutwiler, the scheduler in Houston, tried to train Bush, for months, to say: "Margaret's the one who handles my schedule." They couldn't let a friend even *talk* to Bush . . . because Bush would start fretting about ol' Fitzy in San Francisco, or Binky in Cleveland ("Well, God . . . Binky—shit, he's been so *good* to me—maybe we could blow off that Chicago lunch!") . . . and he'd fly halfway across the country and back to show up under a tent in Binky's backyard.

The fact was, he didn't mind: the endless miles, the eight-event days—he liked the athletic feel of the race. If they made their motel at midnight, with just hours to collapse till the next event . . . it was Bush who'd show up with coffee for the troops at six A.M. If they made their last plane at nine thirty P.M., with nothing but another airport, another long car ride, another motel ahead . . . it was Bush who'd buoy them with his boyish routine: "Tray tables down!" he'd bark, like he used to run the flight-check in his TBM Avenger. "Note paper out! . . . List! . . . Pen! . . . Commence!" If they ended, by chance, at a decent hotel, Bush would stroll the suite, noting aloud each luxury appurtenance. He'd end up at the door to his room, where, with a hint of a bow, he'd announce: "Batesy, I hope this is adequate to your needs."

In Iowa alone, there were ninety-nine counties, and he was organized in every one. He worked *every* Kiwanis, Moose Lodge,

Legion Hall, VFW . . . he worked chicken barbecues, ladies' auctions, cattle barns, farmyards . . . he toured packing houses. He held ("Jeez, warm little critters, aren't they?") *piglets*!

And he made speeches, hundreds—actually, the same speech hundreds of times, a conservative speech about American strength . . . in the world: how Carter let U.S. interests slip away by his moralistic fixation on human rights . . . in the economy: how the nation's vitality was sapped by inflation and overblown government spending . . . in energy: how energy companies had to be unshackled to explore and exploit . . . in intelligence: how a Bush Presidency would beef up the CIA and back it against its critics. (He started by playing down his connection to the Agency, but then he heard the applause when his devotion slipped out one day—after that, there was no speech without mention of the CIA.)

And that led him to his own life—or at least to his résumé. Here, too, Bush was conservative—he didn't give much away. The point of the litany was that he'd *had* all those jobs, *been* all those things ("A President We Won't Have to Train!") . . . not the effect of those jobs on him. The lessons he did adduce were conventional, or conventionally expressed: the CIA taught him *how the world really was* . . . China showed the *blessings of freedom we take for granted.* . . .

Despite the drill of repetition, despite visits to a speech coach (four hours at a stretch with a woman in New York—thousand bucks an hour!), Bush never became a great speaker. He could not really haul his listeners into his life. He did stop pointing with every phrase . . . but now he'd mash the air with spasmic karate chops, or grab fistfuls of air and hold them to his breast to show how much he *meant* those words, or these, which his voice, arising, was *about* to strain forth into that mike. . . .

But at the scale that Iowa offered—forty, fifty folks in a room—what they could see, or, precisely, feel, was his endless energy, the intensity of his want . . . wanting to know them.

"I *know* about the cycle of seasons—the snow, the green, the upturned fields . . . your sense of family. These things will make me a better President. I just *know* it."

What they could feel—especially when they met him, one-on-one (Bush always tried to stay, to meet them)—was his rising confidence in his organization, in himself . . . it was working! He could sense the momentum, the shift . . . he could feel his time, feel the world, come to him! He couldn't tell them how yet—the reporters, the pols, the Washington-wise who came out to Iowa—he just knew it was working.

And in that final winter, when Rich Bond and the boys brought the phones to fever, and all those County Chairmen got their captains out, and the buses lined up to bring the Bush Brigades to the big straw votes . . . they clawed past Ronald Reagan as if he were standing still—Bush won every straw poll! . . . Well, then, everyone could see. This guy had more than a hope. This was a guy to watch! (And such a nice guy—you know, they met him, they rode with him in that Oldsmobile, Bush made them so comfortable!) . . . This guy *was* special! This guy was a *winner.* This could be The One.

That's when Jim Baker and Teeter told him he had to *define himself.* He had to start giving people a clearer idea of what Bush believed in . . . what President Bush would do.

"I don't know," Bush said. "I don't get the feeling people want that."

They argued . . . but Bush just wouldn't believe it. *Personal quality* was his "thing." He thought people would *see* it . . . once they took a look at him.

The fact was, he hadn't a clue how to define himself. Some people saw him as moderate . . . some, conservative—that was fine! He didn't want to rope himself into . . . *positions.*

Why should he?

The fact was, he wanted to *be* President. He didn't want to be President to *do* this or that. He'd do . . . what was *sound.*

When people would ask—reporters, usually—*why* did he want to be President, he'd talk about Big Pres: "My father inculcated the idea of service."

True enough. But one could serve by raising money for United Way. Why President?

One time, a reporter kept asking. Bush said: "Well, you know . . . doesn't everybody grow up wanting to be President?"

Maybe where he grew up.

Anyway, Bush beat Reagan by two percentage points in Iowa, 1980 . . . he got the bounce. He got Big Mo. He never did define himself. So it was in New Hampshire, 1980, that Reagan started painting the picture *for* Bush—a portrait Bush could not live down.

⁂

BUSH WAS EVERYWHERE AFTER he won Iowa—shot up twenty-five percent in the polls. Bush versus Reagan—that was *the* story.

"There is a widespread perception," *The Washington Post* reported, "that Reagan is fading fast."

That's why Reagan arranged to debate Bush, one-on-one—the *Nashua Telegraph* would sponsor the event. It was recognition that the race had boiled down to two men—why not make the face-off fact? Just two guys on stage at the local high school, Saturday night, three days before the vote.

It was high electoral theater.

And the last straw for Dole.

How could they freeze him out? How could they act like Bob Dole didn't exist? Dole, Howard Baker, Phil Crane, John Anderson . . . were they non-candidates?

Dole peppered the papers with angry quotes about Bush—the "Rockefeller candidate" . . . who was "hired help for the big banks" . . . "a member of the Trilateral Commission!" (Bill Loeb, publisher of the *Union Leader*, was happy to retail the slurs.) . . . Dole-lawyers filed complaints with the Federal Election Commission to stop the *Nashua Telegraph* debate. The newspaper had to pull out as sponsor. But Ronald Reagan picked up the costs.

At that point, Dole began calling the other campaigns, working out an ambush. They would *all* show up at the high school—force a showdown, right there on TV—let Bush *try* to keep them out . . . while the whole state watched.

The beauty part was, Reagan's people were in on it! John Sears, Reagan's number-one man, helped script the drama. Dole sent his young advance kid, Mari Maseng, to find a holding room for the four excluded candidates, and someplace they could talk to the press. By phone from his Manchester hotel, Dole worked the details with relish. How long was that hallway to the stage? Where would Bush be sitting?

On the night of the debate, there were fifteen hundred people in the high school gym. Jon Breen, the *Telegraph* editor, moderator of the debate, was shuttling between the Reagan and Bush gangs, trying to work out what to do about Dole, Anderson, Crane, Baker . . . four candidates had invaded! Would George Bush accept their participation?

Bush refused even to *talk* to those guys—this was his shot at Reagan! Rules are rules!

They sent New Hampshire's Senator Gordon Humphrey to reason with Bush: "George, give 'em a chance. It'll be good for the Party!"

"Don't lecture me about the GOP," Bush snapped. "I've worked a lot harder than you have to build the Republican Party."

In the gym, the crowd was yelling—the debate was forty minutes late. Finally, Bush came onstage, smiling and waving. Reagan appeared, to cheers from his faithful. . . . But then the *other* four guys filed in, behind the desks, like spectres from a Dickens tale. The moderator, Breen, announced that he meant to stick to the rules—this would be a two-man debate.

Governor Reagan started a speech—how everybody ought to be included. Breen instructed the technicians to turn off Reagan's mike. That's when Reagan started yelling—he was beautiful! A line from an old movie: "I paid for this microphone, Mr. Green!"

The crowd cheered—even Bush supporters cheered. The other four guys onstage started clapping, waving to the crowd.

Breen was trying to get them offstage. The crowd was yelling. Reagan gracefully stood, and shook all the other fellows' hands as they left. But Bush froze, like a kid who'd rather take his ball and go home. He sat there steaming, couldn't say a word. . . . He looked like a perfect weenie.

Well, Bush got his debate with Reagan—but no one remembered anything they said. What they remembered was that gorgeous Reagan moment ("I paid for this microphone!") . . . and maybe a couple of lines from the press conference Dole arranged in a schoolroom.

Howard Baker said of George Bush: "If he is the front-runner, he wears the crown most unbecomingly."

Dole, as usual, was more direct: "As far as George Bush is concerned, he'd better find himself another Party."

Bush was so rattled he left the state—went to Houston for two days, to "rest" before the New Hampshire vote. Meanwhile, in those two days, Reagan bounced past Bush in the polls. Bush lost New Hampshire . . . and Big Mo. Ultimately, he lost any chance to unhorse Ronald Reagan.

Worse still, he left behind an image of George Bush as a wimp extraordinaire—a stickler for form who choked when it counted. It was a portrait that would haunt him for a decade, a gift from the Gipper (who would never forget how *Bush just sat there*) . . . and from Bob Dole, who wanted Bush to know that the damage would not be confined to that night—nor even to that campaign.

"George!" Dole rasped as he left that stage in Nashua. "There'll be another time."

9

It takes a special man to enjoy the Vice Presidency, but George Bush was the man for the job.

George and Bar decided without even talking: they were going to *like* the Reagans. And they did, right away. They *loved* the Reagans. The only surprise, Bush told his old friends, was how easy it was. Reagan turned out to be a great guy! The way he told those funny stories! You *had* to like the guy.

But it wouldn't have mattered if there had been no charming jokes, if Reagan had been a vicious drooler; just as it did not matter that Reagan had no talent for friendship, no personal connections apart from Nancy. In fact, Reagan couldn't remember his grandchildren's names, and he had no friends, only the husbands of Nancy's friends. It didn't matter! Bush had the talent, a genius for friendship. And like every genius, he worked at it: if Ronald Reagan connected with others solely by means of funny stories, George Bush would bring him funny stories. In fact, the Vice President's staff knew he didn't want briefing memos for the weekly lunch with Reagan: the way to earn a stripe in the OVP was to give him *a joke for the President*. This was no laughing matter to Bush. It was the core of his life's method. Back in 1978, when George Bush was an obscure ex-CIA chief, just starting to run for President, someone asked him: What made Bush think he could be President? "Well," Bush said, without pause, "I've got a big family, and *lots* of friends." Later in that campaign, he learned the "proper" answer, some mumbo jumbo about experience, entrepreneurship, philosophy of government. . . . But the first answer was true. George Bush was trying to become President by making friends, one by one if need be, and Ronald Reagan was a Big One.

It certainly didn't matter that they disagreed—that Voodoo Economics thing, and a few other differences, on civil rights, the environment, education, energy, and U.S. policy on Asia, Africa, Latin America, and Soviet relations. Of course they disagreed, because George Bush knew five times more about the governments of the world—his own included—than Ronald Reagan ever would. But it didn't matter! The fact is, they didn't disagree anymore, because George Bush would not disagree with the President. This was another of George Bush's talents: accommodation. He had the capacity to act on the judgments of others, to live within the bounds of received wisdom. It was a talent that had smoothed his path from his parents' home, through prep school and the U.S. Navy, where the lessons of life were delivered explicitly, and later through Yale, business, and politics, where things grew murkier, and the judgments one lived by had to be doped out. But he did divine them: he was always sensitive to the ethic around him. And to the extent he could accommodate himself, he flourished, and made friends every step of the way. In 1964, he first ran for Senate as a Goldwater man, and though Bush lost, Goldwater was still a friend twenty-two years later. In 1966, for a House seat from Houston, he ran as a Main Street Republican, then served and voted with the moderate mainstream, as a backer of Richard Nixon. And in 1970, when he ran and lost for Senate again (this time, slightly to the left of his rival), he asked his Big Friend, President Nixon, for a job at the UN, which he'd roundly reviled as a Goldwater man. By 1980, the accommodation to Ronald Reagan was just a walk in the park.

And it did not matter if the Reaganauts couldn't see him as one of their own. They screwed most of his friends out of jobs, stopped talking when he came into the room, made jokes about him when he was absent. He knew it, just as surely as Lyndon Johnson had known it about the Kennedys. Hell, it didn't take a rocket scientist to figure it out, the way reporters would ask his staff: "People, uh, in the Cabinet meetings tell me Bush never says anything. . . . Is that true?" Or they'd just print it: "Administration sources said the Vice President had nothing to contribute. . . ." Of course he knew who the sources were. Some were the same hypocrites who came to his office *before* the meeting, asking him to back their schemes, talk to the President for them. . . . Then, when he wouldn't, they'd have some columnist in for breakfast and, just in passing, smiling, with a wedge of grapefruit on their spoons, they'd saw Bush off at the knees. Oh, he knew the game! Still, he never got into that White House cockfight: an eye for an eye, a leak for a leak. Could have had a pro, Jimmy Baker, do it for him. But he wouldn't: it was a matter of loyalty to the team, loyalty to the President; most of all, a matter of discipline.

This was another of Bush's great talents: personal discipline. There were no leaks from the OVP: there was *not one story* saying George Bush was unhappy with this or that decision, or the President overrode objections from George Bush. In fact, there were no stories suggesting Bush had opinions at all, even before a decision came down, even when it would have gotten him off the hook. It would have been so easy: when Ed Meese was filling Reagan's ear with some Neanderthal antiblack screed, sticking the administration's nose into a civil rights fight, putting them all in the soup . . . on the *wrong side* of the issue! And here's a reporter in Bush's armchair, gently inviting: "Mr. Vice President, it seems that you might be less comfortable with something like this. . . ." But Bush wouldn't bite. Never. Christ, the reporters were easy. One of his own aunts came at him, drove him right out of his chair, trying to have a *serious discussion*—why Ronald Reagan refused to have arms talks with the Russians. Years later, she was still half-convinced Bush was willfully stupid, or had the attention span of an eight-year-old. Didn't matter. They could all think so, and he wouldn't lift a finger to prove them wrong. He wouldn't even let his staff help. His first chief of staff, Admiral Daniel Murphy, used to haul every staffer in for a talk, to let them know they had only one job: to help George Bush do *his* job, and *his* job was to help the President. There would be no disagreement between members of the Vice President's staff and the President's staff. They *could not argue with anyone in the White House*. Admiral Dan had them all in, down to the girls who'd answer the phones. And with the same flair he'd once shown as Commander of the Sixth Fleet, he'd warn:

"Honey, tonight you're gonna to go out with your boyfriend. And you're gonna go to a bar, and you're gonna have a drink. And you're gonna want to tell him want a *wonderful* guy you're working for, and what a *great thing* he did today. . . . and how he saved the President from the *most awful thing* that somebody else was trying to do. . . . Sweetheart, you don't know who's in the next booth, do you? So . . . DON'T SAY A GODDAMN THING!"

It got so the whole OVP was a whisper zone in that gray granite building across the street from the White House. People and paper moved back and forth down the dark, lofty halls of the Old EOB—earnest young people, of good families, sons and daughters of George Bush's friends, would *run* between the offices, flushed with the press of business for the Vice President. And nothing came out! George Bush would go out to speak, all over the country, twenty, twenty-five days a month (he wouldn't duck a chance to help the party, the President) . . . and nothing would be heard of him! True, the speeches weren't about George Bush, or what he was doing, or what he thought. They weren't about anything, really, except what a great country, and a great President, we had. That was fine with Bush. All the positions, all the speeches, were just politics to him. The rest, the friendships, or loyalty to the President, those were personal matters— matters of the personal code. That was where Bush's talents lay, and the only thread of steel running through his life to his seventh decade. He wasn't going to let politics change the *way he was.* God forbid! It was all personal with George Bush. He couldn't see things any other way.

Of course, he would accommodate. After he came off like such a stiff in the '84 reelection, and his personal polls took a dive, and reporters on his plane got so nasty, then his friends ganged up and made him change the staff: they told him he had to, if he ever wanted to be President; they called it a more "political" support team. That's when he signed on Lee Atwater—neither son nor friend to any old Bush-friend—to run the PAC and the campaign to come. That's when he had to let Dan Murphy go, and hire Craig Fuller as the new Chief of Staff. Fuller was a young White House pro: neat, calm, organized, and people said he knew how to stick the knife, if he had to. But he was another stranger. Jeez, Bush would call the office now, and half the people who answered were strangers! He'd live with it, if that's what it took. But it just wasn't . . . friendly. And it wasn't really fair to Dan. Those rules weren't Dan's rules, they were Bush's. Bush told him just how he meant to do the job, even before he got elected. It was the fall of '80, at the same lunch where he offered Dan the job. Murphy had been his deputy at the CIA. They could talk frankly. And Bush told him point-blank, wanted him to know how it was going to be, had to be. . . .

"I've thought a lot about it," Bush said. "I know I'm not gonna have much input on policy, nothing substantive to do at all . . .

"And I've decided, I can be happy with that."

And he had been happy. That's what no one could get through their heads, except Bar, of course. That's one of the reasons he loved her: she understood things without talking. She was better at it than he was!

What was the Vice Presidency?

A wonderful adventure.

He had decided—they had decided—that it would be, just as he had decided how he was going to do the job. This was the ultimate triumph of discipline, and George Bush's greatest talent: the power of mind-set. He could decide—they could decide—how it was going to be, and then it *was that way* . . . because no one, *no one*, would ever see them treating it any other way.

They loved the Reagans.

Why?

Because they *loved the Reagans*. They had decided.

And it didn't start in 1980. Talent like that comes from a lifetime. There was the time George Bush's career picked them up and moved them to Houston, and the wife of a business friend gave a tea for Barbara, to show her off to the ladies.

So they came to meet her, and one after the other, they asked: "And where do *you* come from?"

Bar said sweetly: "I live in Houston now."

"Oh. Yes, but . . . where do you *come* from?"

And Bar, with her smile still placid, beatific, replied: "Houston is my home now."

They weren't going to put her in that box, thank you. And they weren't going to hand her husband a carpetbag, either. She had decided.

But the brilliance of it was, it wasn't one party, one lunch with Admiral Dan, or one talk to the staff. It was there every day, unwavering.

What is the Vice Presidency?

A wonderful adventure. Every day.

10

George Bush did not know why he couldn't feel it. He'd won ... he'd wiped the field clean! He'd won every state in Super Tuesday—a *shutout* ... and never had to break a sweat in Illinois. . . . Wisconsin—no contest—Dole just hung in for one more week, to make a speech, have his say . . . Bush could understand that. He understood too well. "Dole must be tired," he said. "It's hard to snap back . . . feels like a death in the family."

It was hard for Bush to snap back . . . or snap *to* the fact that he'd won. The course he'd been running for ten years was at an end—he was the nominee. Let go that baton! Take a bow!

Friends told him, Super Tuesday night: Hey! It's over—done deal!

"I just don't see that," Bush said. "I don't feel that. I don't want to feel that. If I felt that, I'd do something wrong, or I'd react in a bad way . . . not working hard, or whatever it is."

So he went on to Illinois and vowed that no one would work harder. He acted like he was holding on for dear life—in a way, he was. And he wouldn't give up on Wisconsin—didn't want to hear that it really didn't matter.

It was like a muscle that he couldn't unclench. He won and he won and he won . . . and, at last, he flew back to Washington. They were on the ground at Andrews Air Force Base, and Bush wandered back from the Power Cabin—he came to wish the staff Happy Easter. They wished him congratulations on his victory.

"Somehow," Bush said, "I don't have that . . . exhilaration."

THE WHITE MEN SCHEDULED a rally—in Washington, a full tribal salute. They called it the Over-the-Top Rally . . . it was going to be big. . . . They'd get all these folks to wave signs and scream for Bush—cheer him on toward the Oval Office. And then . . . *then!* . . . from the Oval itself, they would march in the Big Brush-Chopper—the *Gip!*—who would finally be free to drop his pose of disinterest, end his official, statesmanlike neutrality . . . and *at last* . . . for the good of the party, and in tribute to the loyalty of seven years . . . put his shoulder to the wheel for the *one man* he trusted to stand beside him . . . *at last!* . . . Ronald Reagan would endorse George Bush.

So GBFP and the OVP set to work on a Reagan speech about their man . . . beautiful stuff about Bush at the President's elbow, a force for calm, for strength, for decency, for true conservatism! . . . They had pages of praise, all typed up, sent in to the White House writers.

And they held the rally: first week in April, weather just right, crowd big enough—noisy, too—and Bush made a speech, said they were going to *win in November* . . . and he looked like a winner, or deserved to, with all those delegates in his column, the nomination locked up, the party united, everybody behind him . . . almost.

Bush finished speaking, the crowd finished cheering and . . . no Gip.

Where's the President?

No President.

No explanation.

Mercury in retrograde?

LUCKILY, IT DIDN'T MAKE news—the Reagan nonappearance at the big Bush rally. The stuff about Mercury, Uranus, and all . . . that was front-page. Don Regan's book was seeping into the papers, newsmagazines, and TV—TV loved that book! Nancy and the astrologer—*too delicious!* . . . Bush started getting questions on astrology: *What did he know and when did he know it* . . . about Sagittarius rising.

Then, too, there was Attorney General Meese, whose top staff resigned, and he couldn't hire replacements. No one wanted to play in the slush with Ed.

Meanwhile, there was a steady drip, drip, drip . . . from Panama and General Noriega. The Reagan White House wanted Noriega out . . . then it turned out that U.S. intelligence (the CIA, for example, under Director George Bush) had been paying Noriega as a stoolie for years. The Reaganauts contended Noriega was a drug kingpin (Bush insisted he only just found out) . . . then it turned out the Drug Enforcement boys had been awarding Noriega citations of merit! The Reagan Justice Department indicted Noriega in a South Florida court . . . then the Reagan State Department sent legations to tell him: the indictments would be dropped only if he'd take his dirty money and go.

Noriega wouldn't leave Panama.

Meese wouldn't leave the Justice Department.

Don Regan was on every talk show in the country.

Michael Dukakis was hopping from state to state, beating Jesse Jackson every Tuesday and beating up on Bush with "White House astrology" . . . "the sleaze factor" . . . "deals with drug-running Panamanian dictators." Late April, a *Time* magazine poll had Bush eleven points behind Dukakis in a head-to-head race. Early May, Gallup had Bush thirteen down. . . .

Nancy wouldn't let Ronnie out of the house to endorse George Bush. . . . What did it matter? . . . Reagan's polls were at an all-time low, along with his political charm. Reagan was part of Bush's problem.

Which gave the white men an idea: *Hey!* . . . How 'bout if we get Bush to *separate from Reagan?* . . . He could be *his own man!* . . . Say something about Meese?

"No!"

Noriega?

"No!" said George Bush. "I'm not gonna start that now!"

As THE FAMILY LIKED to tell it, George Bush was the calmest hand on deck. Friends were calling from all over the country, wringing their hands and moaning: Why couldn't he *do something?* The Gee-Six, as Bush's white men styled themselves, were in a lather . . . panicky about Dukakis's lead.

Junior knew that, of course, with his office on the Wing of Power. Hell, he was among them enough to worry, too. He knew all the bad news: the polls, the "internals," the "gender gap," the "negatives." He knew the schedule for the next two months held nothing to help Bush get back on the evening news. Dukakis looked like the centrist statesman in his week-to-week wins over Jesse Jackson. He would hold the spotlight through July, as the Democrats convened in Atlanta. George Bush couldn't even throw his own body around the country to get onto *local* TV. . . . GBFP had spent the legal limit; the travel budget was a hundred thousand *overspent* . . . no one wanted to tell the Veep.

Junior talked to his father, just before Memorial Day. He kept it casual—the normal stuff: Laura's fine . . . the kids. . . .

Only at the end, Junior asked: "How are you, Dad? . . . Are you okay with this thing? You think it's all right?"

"Yeah," said George Bush. He sounded surprised by the question. "People don't know who this guy is. . . ."

He meant Dukakis. There was no doubt in Bush's mind what the issue would be in this campaign. And also no doubt: Dukakis had no idea about life in the bubble.

That would make all the difference.

"I mean, who is this guy? . . . You've got to remember, Dukakis has never been here before."

IT ALL WENT BACK to the view from that big house at Walker's Point. All the research, the focus groups, were just detail—*one look* told Bush all he had to know.

In the view from the Point, Dukakis was *obviously* a little outsider (Who *was* he? Where'd he ever *been?*) . . . who did not know the world, as it was to George Bush.

Dukakis was another one-worlder, blame-America-first, UN, World Court, human-rights *liberal* . . . who was going to *give away the store*!

Dukakis was another put-on-a-sweater, turn-down-the-thermostat, fifty-five-mile-an-hour, five-thousand-pages-of-Energy-Department-regs *Governor* . . . who'd try to thin the mixture in the great economic engine.

Dukakis was another brainy tax-and-tinker-technocrat *Democrat* . . . who was going to . . . *screw* . . . *everything* . . . *up*!

Dukakis was . . . *Jimmy Carter.*

That solved a lot of problems for Bush.

Bush could vow that he'd labor to define himself. He'd show the country what he believed in . . . he'd work like the devil on that vision thing. . . . But he wouldn't have to. The Bush campaign would not be—could not be—about nothing . . . as long as it was about Dukakis. *He* shouldn't be President!

From the moment Dukakis appeared in the bombsight, there would be no lack of mission. Bush would protect the heritance!

If the W-word at the Point was Winning . . . if there was only one man to tend the big house . . . if there was, in every *good* family, one in each generation who must be steward . . . then there must be one to take his turn at the helm of the great ship, and steer it on, unharmed, to the shores of well-being. Bush lived his life to be that man.

There was a line that crept into his speeches. It never got famous, like the catchy bluster of "Read my lips!" . . . but people in the crowds would look up when he said it . . . there was such an (unusual) air of conviction in Bush's voice. . . . It came at the end of his praise for Ronald Reagan, how people felt differently about the U.S.A. now . . . how different was the economy, the business climate, the tax code . . . Bush would praise all these supposed achievements, and then say:

"And I'm not going to let them take it away."

There was the mission! There was the message of the campaign, in one line. And that line made perfect sense to Bush— once "them" became Michael Dukakis.

After that, Bush would do . . . whatever it took.

II

THE MOST ELOQUENT SIGN was that his putting came back. Any weekend golfer knows, you hit the long drives with your legs and back, full swing of the arms, turn of the torso—big body action, muscle and mechanics . . . but a dinky four-foot putt puts the mirror to your troubled soul. And Bush . . . well, not to be harsh, but . . . Bush stunk up every green for *eight years* as Vice President. He had the yips.

When he got the nomination wrapped up, he got one of those long semi-legal putters and went out to play . . . that was the first hint. He got back to the big house on the Point and broke in on his sons, who were planning a golf match—"Don't count me out!" . . . After he won the election, he'd stand behind that big putter, and he could see every inch of the path that ball would travel, the hole looked twice as big and . . . bingo! In the cup! That's when he announced to the family, and the world:

"Mr. Smooth . . . is back!"

And through the first couple of months of his administration, you'd barely find anyone to argue. Bush looked so happy in the job—like he knew exactly what he'd find, and he'd just been waiting to sit in that chair, to show the right way to do things . . . it was instantly well-known that this was a transition unlike other transitions. A real insider, said the triple-E pundits—a sure-fingered masseur of Congress and the agencies. A confident and sharing man, said admiring reporters in his press conferences—he took questions about *anything*! You could see him thinking up the answers, *himself.* He didn't have to wait for six months of staff work, he picked up the phone and called Gorby—to chat. This was a man who knew the ropes in the rigging of the great Ship of State.

Of course, that's exactly what Bush meant to show. He laughed off the idea that the job was oversized. Not that he meant to brag—anything but! He'd say something humble, like, the Gipper left the shop in great shape, or the fine people in the government were wonderful about cooperating, or he was lucky enough to have had some experience . . . Mr. Smooth! He looked like he had come to believe his old campaign slogan: "Ready on Day One to Be a Great President."

But there are different ways to become President—not all of them easy to pin down. Bush won the vote, November '88, and became President, politically. He took the oath at the Capitol, January '89, and became president, constitutionally. But it would take time, he knew, before his Presidency, the look and sound of him in that office, could settle into the public mind as fact, when the words "President Bush" would sound easy together, like "Washington" and "D.C."—that date could not be predicted.

Nor could the date of dread and dreams when the nation's fortunes would seem to be at stake, and the people would turn to their president—*to him*—and expect him to act, and to win. Nothing about that moment could be predicted, except . . . that would mark the last becoming—at that moment, for good or ill, the Presidency would descend upon him.

And that was the moment for which Bush waited. When friends gushed to him about approval polls (over sixty percent!), the splendid press he was getting, his graceful (so effortless!) personal success, Bush would say the polls could be fickle. The press would surely turn. As for himself, he'd say, he hadn't yet "been tested by fire."

HE WAS RIGHT ABOUT the polls—they started sliding. In his third month, the Senate killed off his Cabinet nominee John Tower, the first time in thirty years such a slap was dealt to a new President. Hundreds of top-level jobs in the government were still vacant, or filled with Reagan holdovers who were doing the country the service of keeping those paychecks warm. Bush had no major bills before the Congress. He had yet to answer Gorbachev's call for accelerated arms control. The foreign policies of the United States were said to be on hold for mysterious "reviews" by unnamed officials and experts . . . and, sure enough, Bush was being hammered in print.

"A Presidency 'On the Edge of a Cliff' " was the lead essay in *The Washington Post*'s Sunday Outlook section. In it, no less than

David Gergen declared the administration atotter. Bush was a "Mexican Jumping Bean," traveling too much, giving speeches about nothing; he was neglecting the "vision thing" and frittering time on details; he'd stuck with Tower so long he'd created a political bloodbath; he was clueless without his campaign white men, dependent on the lowbrow John Sununu; Bush was "being nibbled and nicked to death," he was too often "surprised," "reactive," "chained to his in-box"—this went on for fifty solid inches . . . and, of course, Gergen was not alone. *Everybody knew* poor Bush was out to lunch. And not just OTL, but egregiously, obtusely, willfully lackadaisical—close to *negligent* (Bush didn't *want* to do anything, well-known people-in-the-know insisted) . . . because everybody had just finished writing (last month) how Bush-the-insider knew everything about being President . . . so how could they turn now and report he was having a hard time?

That was the first time I caught a glimpse of Bush the President. I was in a White House hallway, waiting to go upstairs to see Barbara Bush, when . . . came flying out of a doorway, George Bush, twenty feet away and closing. He had a pack of suits behind him, Secret Service guys and policy guys, the military guy, and who-knows-what guys—twelve, at least, fanned out in his wake, in a ragged V, like Canada geese, pumping their arms to keep up and wearing purposeful scowls, all . . . except for Bush. I murmured to Bar's aide, at my side, "There's the boss!" Bush whipped his head around with a vague smile— trying to locate the source so he could make a goofy face at whoever it was, give that personal gift that had brought him to these great halls—but he had the loose-eyed and inward look of an athlete in the final quarter, deep in the game, everything pumping in him with an internal roar that would dim all outside . . . except, of course, he was George Bush, so the game *was* every person outside—each one, individually, owed a measure of his energy and a tick off his clock, which he was trying to give *(Who was that?)* while he's still the lead goose, couldn't miss a step, because the others would march up his back, and the next meeting (and the next, and the next) couldn't start till he got there, and anyway, he's the *boss*, supposed to be out front . . . all the time.

It seemed to me, Bush wasn't lackadaisical *for one instant*, and all the stray facts that were retailed at lunch tables fell into a pattern of another shape.

President Bush stuck to the bitter end with John Tower, not because he courted (or didn't know enough to avoid) the political showdown . . . but because Captain Poppy stood by his ungainly chum, Ovie, when the rest of the Andover squad would have shooed Ovie off the field.

President Bush had two daily go-rounds with his chief of staff, John Sununu, morning and evening, while Sununu ticked off items from his notebook and Bush knocked them down, one by one (trying to do, with each, whatever seemed sound) . . . not because Sununu, Rasputin-of-the-Rocky-North, had a choke-hold on the President or his agenda . . . but because George Bush was the Harris County Chairman who *always* stopped by the office at night, to read the memos, sign the mail, and clear his desk before he went home to Bar and the kids.

This President charged about the country giving airy,

friendly speeches about nothing-in-particular, not because Sununu was fearful of competition from bright speechwriters, or because this White House was without the political edge of the G-6 . . . but because George Bush ("Watch the *action*!") had risen for forty years in business, politics, and government, *always* on the move, always by the coin of his person—he was practicing the *essence* of his politics, precisely by jumping on a plane and *showing up.*

President Bush picked up the phone to chat with Gorbachev (and Thatcher, Kohl, Mitterrand, Andreotti, Takeshita, Mulroney, Salinas, Aquino, Mubarak, King Hussein, King Hassan, King Fahd, and forty or fifty lesser-known heads of state . . .) because the Commander in Chief and Leader of the Free World was going to save the planet from conflict . . . the same way George Bush saved the county GOP from warfare with the Birchers—by interposing his person: they were all going to like him, he *knew* they would, they were going to be friends.

The horrifying fact was, he didn't know any other way. He was using everything he ever knew—and some things he wished to God he knew better . . . but all he had to go on, all he could bring to the job, was his own life before he hit the bubble. And God knows, he was spending it—pouring it out, to do this job. Mr. Smooth was working his withered old buns off.

AND HEAVEN HELP THE fellow with whom George Bush did not want to be friends—especially if that fellow happened to run some small troublemaking nation, one of those "little wiener countries." The personal coin, like any other, had two sides.

Manuel Noriega, the Panamanian strongman, was once an informant to DCI Bush. In the eighties, Bush knew him as one of the Reaganoids' unsavory anticommie pals. By '86, when Noriega's goons started killing off his opponents, the general became an embarrassment—even to the Gip. Worse still, though the Reaganoids blustered—the Justice Department *indicted* the general, in a U.S. court in Florida—Manuel Noriega refused to leave power!

Worse still, Noriega had shown his most cheeky recalcitrance in the middle of George Bush's campaign.

Noriega may not have known, but his life was dog food. He made his great mistake on December 15, 1989, eleven months into George Bush's term. An off-duty U.S. Marine was shot by Noriega's troops at a roadblock in Panama. At that same roadblock, a Navy lieutenant and his wife were arrested, the man was beaten up, the woman was threatened with sexual assault . . . and that was the end. George Bush was once a young Navy lieutenant, with a young wife . . .

The next day, a Sunday, George Bush broke away from his Christmas party and went upstairs to the White House residence to hear the Pentagon's plans for invasion. Bush had on his bright red socks, one of which said "Merry," and one of which said "Christmas."

Twenty-four thousand U.S. troops would destroy Panama's force of sixteen thousand (only three thousand Panamanians were considered "combat-ready"). The United States would take over the country, depose its government, swear in the new guy, and prop him up while he cleaned up the mess. As for Noriega, they meant to snatch him, and bring him to Miami for trial, like a street criminal.

"Okay," Bush said. "Let's go."

Two years later, there would be millions of words expended about the "emergence" of the Warrior Bush in the Persian Gulf. There would be foreign-affairs dissertations about the way he made *himself* the linchpin of a worldwide alliance against Iraq. There would be high-level semiotic *analysis* of the steps by which Bush *personalized* the war—turned it into a crusade against one man, Saddam Hussein, whom Bush used (so the savants said) as the focus for public enmity, to build support for a war about oil.

Two years later, even Washington people well-known to be in-the-know were amazed (and not a little horrified) to discover the miracle of combat-ardor in this friendly, well-bred President Bush.

But George Bush found the leitmotiv of his administration on Christmas Eve, 1989. He needed no calculation to personalize his combat—or the conduct of alliance. What it took was a lifetime's training—and he had nothing else to throw at a crisis.

U.S. TROOPS SHOT UP Panama in a hurry. They controlled all the strong points and the city streets. They held the water and electric plants, the canal, the bridges and airports. The invasion went better than any God-fearing man would have dared to hope. It was over in one night. By the time the U.S. news crews got there, Panamanians were celebrating in the streets.

But no Noriega.

The second day, the news crews showed looting. And no Noriega.

The third day, weeping Panamanian widows, wounded Americans! Snipers, still firing! . . . And no Noriega.

George Bush had sent twenty-four thousand young Americans in harm's way—twenty-three servicemen were dead. Bush had gone on TV and said the purpose of this extravaganza was . . . to get Noriega.

And he had no Noriega.

The fifth day was Sunday, Christmas Eve . . . the President and family had gathered at Camp David . . . and George Bush was wound so tight that his back seized up—he was hunched, walking like a hundred-and-eight-year-old man. *Where was that sonofabitch Noriega?* Was he headed for the hills like Augusto Sandino? Was George Bush going to spend months—*years?*—greeting body bags at Dover AFB?

It got so bad with Bush's back, he couldn't even play *sports* with his sons. He didn't sideline easy when a game was on the line, but . . . Mr. Smooth couldn't even stand up.

So it came to pass, that Christmas Eve, Bush was standing on the white-tiled balcony of the squash court. (The game at hand was wally-ball—a volleyball, rocketing around a closed court—fast, and rough.) And all Bush could do was watch his sons, George W., Jeb, Neil, and Marvin, dividing into teams, with a couple of Marines, contesting for the wally-ball *championship* of the Camp, and the clan. It was a tight match—hard fought, long, and near its brutal climax . . . when the phone on the balcony rang.

George Bush talked on the phone for a minute . . . and then he was back at the rail of the balcony. Suddenly six-foot-two again, looming on his clean white perch over the white court, George Bush held up one hand to still the game below.

"Noriega," he said, "has given up to the Papal Nuncio in Panama."

And with that, the entire male line of the Bush clan let the ball bounce to standstill on the gleaming white floor, and . . . looking up at the white balcony, applauded their father, who had become President.

ABOUT THE AUTHOR

RICHARD BEN CRAMER (1950–2013) won a Pulitzer Prize for *The Philadelphia Inquirer* in 1979, and his epic work *What It Takes* has been widely hailed as one of the finest books about American politics ever written. He was also the bestselling author of *Joe DiMaggio: The Hero's Life*, *What Do You Think of Ted Williams Now?*, *Ted Williams: The Seasons of the Kid*, and *How Israel Lost*.